W9-BCV-550

Migrations
The IRISH
at Home & Abroad

BY THE SAME AUTHOR

Transitions: Narratives in Modern Irish Culture
(Wolfhound Press, 1987; Manchester U.P. 1988)

Poétique du Possible
(Beauchesne, Paris, 1984)

Myth and Motherland
(Field Day Publications, 1984)

Modern Movements in European Philosophy
(Manchester U.P. 1986)

The Wake of Imagination
(Hutchinson, 1987)

EDITED AND COEDITED BY THE SAME AUTHOR

The Black Book: An Analysis of 3rd Level Education
(Denam Press, Dublin, 1977)

Heidegger et la Question de Dieu
(Grasset, Paris, 1981)

The Crane Bag Book of Irish Studies
(Blackwater Press, Dublin, 1982)

The Irish Mind: Exploring Intellectual Traditions
(Wolfhound Press, 1985)

The Crane Bag Book of Irish Studies, Volume 2
(Wolfhound Press, 1987)

Migrations
The IRISH
at Home & Abroad

Edited by
Richard Kearney

WOLFHOUND PRESS

© 1990 Richard Kearney
Texts © Individual authors

All rights reserved. No part of this book may be reproduced or utilised in any form or by any means, electronic or mechanical, including photography, filming, recording, video recording, photocopying or by any information storage and retrieval system, or otherwise circulated in any form of binding or cover other than that in which it is published, without prior permission in writing from the publisher.

First published 1990 by
WOLFHOUND PRESS
68 Mountjoy Square,
Dublin 1.

ISBN 0-86327-236-3

Wolfhound Press receives financial assistance from
The Arts Council (An Chomhairle Ealaíon), Dublin, Ireland.

Cover design: Jan de Fouw
Cover illustration: From the Series 'People Looking at Paintings'
   by Robert Ballagh
Typesetting: Redsetter Ltd., Dublin.
Printed in Ireland by Colour Books Ltd.

CONTENTS

CONTRIBUTORS

RICHARD KEARNEY: Professor of Philosophy, University College Dublin. Editor of *The Irish Mind*, co-editor of *The Crane Bag*, author of *Transitions* and *The Wake of the Imagination*, selected as one of *Choice's* outstanding academic books of the year 1989.

MAURICE HAYES: Northern Ireland Ombudsman. Member of the Standing Advisory Committee on Human Rights. Former Permanent Secretary of the Department of Health and Social Services. First chairman of the Northern Ireland Community Relations Committee.

SEAMUS HEANEY: Poet. Boylston Chair of Rhetoric and Logic, and Oxford Professor of Poetry. *The Haw Lantern* (Faber, 1988) is his most recent collection.

JOSEPH J. LEE: Professor of Modern History at University College, Cork. Author of *Ireland 1912-1985: Politics and Society* (C.U.P., 1990).

LIAM RYAN: Professor of Sociology at St. Patrick's College, Maynooth. Author of *Attitudes and Values in Ireland*.

GEORGE QUIGLEY: Chairman of the Ulster Bank. Former Permanent Secretary of Northern Ireland Department of Finance. Chairman of the Institute of Directors, Northern Ireland. Member of the Fair Employment Commission.

GRAEME KIRKHAM: Lecturer in History, University of Ulster at Coleraine. A specialist in the field of emigration.

KERBY A. MILLER: Professor of History at the University of Missouri, Columbia. Author of *Emigrants & Exiles: Ireland and the Irish Exodus to North America* (OUP, 1985).

Editor's Note

Somebody once recommended that Ireland's infamous problem of identity might best be resolved in a *ménage-à-trois*. The suggestion was, I believe, that such an adventurous triangle would afford Ireland the opportunity to supersede its ancient quarrel with its closest neighbour in favour of an ampler 'totality of relationships'. The prospect of a more integrated liaison with the newly emerging Europe together with a more cohesive bond with the 'extended Irish family' in overseas continents, offers considerable grounds for hope. But to speak of the international Irish community abroad makes little sense without an equally weighted allegiance to the Irish communities at home. One of the signal achievements of the Ireland Funds has been to reconnect a *global* sense of becoming with a *local* sense of being. And to have done so in a way which extends and revises the conventional models of *national* self-understanding.

Much has been written about Ireland's national identity; and by implication our national difference from England – that country we love to hate yet never cease to imitate, as our first President, Douglas Hyde, remarked. In the process, Ireland's extra-national relations have frequently been neglected. These include both our belonging to international communities beyond the nation-state and to regional communities within it. One of the consequences of such neglect has been a tendency to resort to an insular, enclosed and exclusive sense of identity.

The essays in this collection serve, in different ways, to re-establish some kind of balance between the three partners of Irish communal allegiance: the *regional*, the *national*, and the *global*. Some focus on the triumphs and tribulations of emigration; others on the rites of homecoming. But all share a common concern with the crisis of identity which has found echoes, over the centuries, in our vexed 'national question'. These papers gesture towards ways of acknowledging our identity through difference – the diversity of communities inhabiting this island as well as the multiple migrations to and from other communities abroad.

I would like to express gratitude not only to the contributors to this volume but also to A. J. F. O'Reilly, Chairman of the Ireland Funds and to Judy Hayes, Director of its Advisory Committee, for providing the occasion for these reflections on the Irish community at home and abroad.

Richard Kearney

'Migratory Birds and Roundy Heads'

MAURICE HAYES

Chairman's Introduction

The papers printed in this volume were presented at successive annual conferences of the Ireland Funds in 1988 and 1989.

The Ireland Funds comprise a federation of independent Ireland Funds in America, Canada, Australia and Great Britain with the recent addition of France. Each is an independent charitable foundation in its own country raising money for the purposes of the Ireland Funds.

The pathfinder in this operation was the American Ireland Fund, established in 1976, mainly through the initiative of Dr. A. J. F. O'Reilly, and incorporating, since 1987, the American Irish Foundation which had been set up in 1963 as a result of an initiative by President de Valera and President John F. Kennedy.

The grant making philosophy of the Funds is focused on the trinity of peace, culture and charity, and includes programmes for cross-community reconciliation, education, micro-enterprise and youth. The Funds encourage indigenous community developments at the social, cultural and economic level. In Northern Ireland where development in these areas has been polarised between the communities, the Ireland Funds, committed to a policy of reconciliation and integration, strive to nurture a peaceful and fruitful co-existence in which both nationalist and unionist identities are mutually respected.

The combined Boards of the separate Funds hold an annual meeting in Ireland. As a prelude to this meeting, to inform the Board members of social economic and cultural trends in Ireland, and to provide a context in which they can take strategic decisions on funding policy, the conference has traditionally been broadened to include academics, creative writers and artists, community workers and others as well as the Funds' Irish Advisory Committee and some of those who have received grants. All these people make an input to the conference either in the formal sessions or less formally. Some present papers as a stimulus to debate and discussion in which all participate. The papers in this volume were presented in this way and I had the good fortune and the very great pleasure to chair the discussions on both occasions. Neither I as Chairman, nor the authors, are members of, or otherwise connected with the Funds. We were given freedom to express our views in our own way, subject only to challenge in the subsequent debate. The views expressed are those of the individual speakers, and for this the Ireland Funds carry no responsibility. Neither do we carry responsibility for any conclusions they may have drawn, individually or corporately, from the proceedings, or from any funding decisions that flow from them.

These paragraphs are based on the Chairman's introductory remarks to the Conferences, and are intended to provide no more than a minimal contextual framework for the essays which follow.

The papers were intended to raise questions, rather than to provide answers. The discussions are exploratory rather than definitive. No conclusions were drawn, no votes taken, no consensus demanded. The papers are what they are – a contribution to a debate, loosely linked around a theme: no more than that. They are, at best, a series of illustrative snap-shots. They are not intended as an encyclopaedic review of the subject. They do not presume to provide all the answers. Indeed, they may well not provide any.

The intention in 1988 was to examine the processes of emigration from Ireland, both historically and as a current social phenomenon. The debate spilled over into the 1989 conference where the emphasis was rather more on the performance of the Irish at home.

Emigration is a fascinating and complex topic for any Irish audience. It was especially so for one containing so many well-heeled members of the diaspora, hardly a random sample, it is true, of the Irish abroad (or at home) but sufficiently committed to the common weal to devote two summer's days to the discussion.

The bridge between the two discussions was provided by a

seminal contribution by Seamus Heaney. His characterisation of the doubleness of focus in Ireland, a capacity for being in two places at one time or in two times in one place, a capacity shared by all traditions on the island, which enables them to acknowledge the claims of contradicting truths without having to choose between them, was a profound illumination of the theme of the conference. Specifically, he used a figure to explain the collision (or failure to collide) of the puritan vision of de Valera and the pragmatism of Lemass, and the impact of an international commercial culture on a society which prided itself on its nonmaterialistic values. He illustrated this ability to live in two worlds, this tension between imagined truths and ordered existence in a memorable description of two Cork school-boys, writing differently, swinging from the prosaic correctness of received school English to the barely remembered excitement of a dialect phrase: 'The swallow is a migratory bird: he have a roundy head.'

In a way, the conferences were about both migratory birds and roundy heads, with echoes of Hopkins' 'roundy wells in which stones ring', or to shift the metaphor to another time and another country, of roundheads and cavaliers with the emigrants cast as cavaliers and the stay at homes as roundheads.

Nothing exemplifies this two-timing Irish mind better than our attitude to emigration which is capable of being portrayed as both triumph and disaster: on the one hand the Irish taking over the world, on the other the Irish banished and expelled from their own land by political, religious or economic oppression. The one cherishes every slight, every historic injury, every actual or supposed wrong as a weapon with which to assail the perceived oppressor, or as an excuse to explain the sad condition of modern Ireland. The other scans the world's press for a name which could be Irish, no matter by how many generations removed, for sign of an Irishman doing well in foreign fields.

I knew one loyal Kerry woman who went to her grave believing that Marshal Timoshenko, of the Red Army, the defender of Moscow and Smolensk, was the son of Tim O'Shea of Dromin who had run off with a Russian circus in the second year of the Boer War, and that Tom Crean would have brought Scott back from the South Pole if only he had had the wit to take him.

In a way, we always seem to have been at it. The early Celtic

tales are all about movement, of migration into Ireland – as in
the Leabhar Gabhála, or around the country, as in the Táin and
the Fiannaíocht. The emergence of the Immram, too, the
voyages of Bran and Brendan and others, can be no accident–
the fusion of an inherited obsession with travel with a missionary
zeal illustrated by wonder tales of mystery and imagination.
Perhaps this propensity to movement is genetically determined.
If there is a Celtic thing it seems to have been characterised by
restlessness, both of mind and body. In their day they seemed to
be all over the place limited only by the constraints of contemporary transport technologies. There is an almost Heraclitean
sense of movement, of everything being in flux, which may well
have left a mark on the Irish psyche. One can feel, too, the sense
of a wave rolling across Europe from the Caspian to the Atlantic
over the first five or six centuries of the Christian era, and it is not
too fanciful to see the continuation of this movement across the
American continent in the 18th and 19th centuries. There is
another view which sees the Celts in their Irish or Scotch-Irish
variants as the eternal frontiersmen until they ran out of road in
the Yukon. They can be characterised, too, as a congenital irrit-
ant, a stone in the shoe of society whereon they went.

It may be this compulsion to movement that Seamus Heaney
had in mind when he wrote:

> 'We are a dispersed people, whose history
> is a sensation of opaque fidelity.'

For those of us brought up on 19th century historiography and
embedded folklore and legend, emigration broke down into
three clear phases, one golden and glorious, one silver but
salvable and one leaden, debased and rapidly losing value. The
first was the period in which the Irish monks carried the Christian faith and the basic values of western civilisation back to the
Continent. I grew up in Downpatrick, where, on St Patrick's
Day each year, an eccentric curate began his address with the
words 'Here in this Church, the head and mother Church of all
the Churches in the English-speaking world' which did a lot for
our sense of local pride! One was aware, too, in that district of
Gall and Columbanus, and the peregrini pro Christi – of connec-
tions being made and parallels drawn with modern missionary

efforts in China and Africa and some suggestion that this was what young Catholic boys were put in the world for (and in any case it was easier than looking for a job in Belfast). It was only much later that I came to know and enjoy the lapsed secular wing of this monastic caravanserai – the troubadours, jongleurs and clerical con-men immortalised by Helen Waddell in *The Wandering Scholars*.

From this it was, in video terms, fast forward to the 17th and 18th centuries, to a version of the 17th century, the product of 18th century aisling poetry and 19th century romantic history. Mac an Cheannaí perpetually in a state of temporary exile, waiting for the opportunity to remove Gráinne Mhaol from the oppressor. Or more gloriously even, the Flight of the Earls, the Wild Geese. 'On far foreign fields from Dunkirk to Belgrade', 'O that this were for Ireland'.

It was only much later that I came to a view that some at least of these were the White Russians of their day, contracting gout and unnameable varieties of pox in the courts of Europe while leaving a leaderless and persecuted peasantry in their wake. Unfair as it might be to the Waddings and Aodh Mac Aingil (the 'Bráithrín bocht ó Dhún') and to many thousands of others, for my present purposes it is the perception that is important, and the perception was romanticised, swashbuckling – and linked with ultimate defeat. Modern research, too, has shown a much less black and white picture than either the full rigours of penal oppression or Daniel Corkery's *Hidden Ireland*, a more complex system of land holding, more movement backwards and forwards to Europe, and more continuity in social life. Perhaps the real heroes were those who stayed.

And then there was emigration to America – all post-famine and crowbar brigades and coffin ships where penal laws merged into want, fever and starvation and land evictions in the race memory. And the other side of the coin: all our guys, out there, doing well in ways denied to them at home.

It was a considerable shock to have Terence O'Neill announce that the Scots-Irish were at it first, and had supplied battalions of Presidents and founding fathers. That, in fact, as Donald Akenson has shown, before the Great Famine, Irish Catholics and Protestants emigrated in almost equal numbers.

Oddly enough movement to England, of which there was a

great deal, was hardly seen as emigration at all, to Scotland, not at all. Perhaps England was too near for emigration to be regarded as irrevocable (although for most it was). Perhaps Australia was too far – the bourn from which no traveller returns. This fixation with North America, and particularly the United States, is interesting. This was the real emigration – travel to Europe hardly qualified at all. Going to England carried a stigma of failure that was not associated with America. The local paper often carried reports of magistrates giving petty offenders the option of a fine or prison, or going to England. The States, on the other hand, was the place for heroes either in Hollywood glamour or Jimmy Cagney toughness or decent Irish cops or kindly but muscular priests.

It is something of a corrective, then, that some of the conference papers focus on emigration to England, Australia or Canada as well as to the United States.

Most of the time, however, far off fields were indeed green, the land of opportunity was far away across the sea, and since only the successful came back to tell, success was seen to be the norm.

I wonder, often, what the psychological effect of this view of emigration was. If the best were seen to be abroad, 'Dá dtagadís na feara chughainn d'imigh uainn sa Spáinn', it didn't do much for the morale of those who remained. If deliverance was always going to come from abroad, if Irishmen could only prosper abroad, this had a queerly enervating effect on those left at home. In a Darwinian sense it was a survival of the weakest. Again, in a Heraclitean echo, 'becoming' was more important than 'being', 'queerly subjunctive', what Seamus Heaney has identified as 'a land of optative moods'. The best had gone – to a better place. Those with get up and go had got up and gone. And this, I think, sowed the seeds of communal escapism. Emigration, or the view of the emigrant as successful, promised a better life, compensation for disadvantage, discrimination, inequality of opportunity and lack of success in this one. In a way, emigration was the opium of the Taigs.

Whatever the reasons, the effect, particularly of 19th century emigration, has been to leave the Irish one of the most internationally dispersed of the European national cultures, a process that seems to be going on with the current rate of emigration

where almost the same numbers leave the Republic each year as
are born there and there is substantial, if less clearly quantified,
movement out of Northern Ireland.

All of which reminded us, approximately two days after
Bloomsday, of Leopold Bloom's description of a Nation as
'People, you know, living in the same place' and then, when
challenged, conveniently extending the definition: 'And also
living in different places'. So to MacMorris' question 'What ish
my nation?' we must add 'Where ish my nation?'.

The conference went on to examine some aspects of what the
Irish did in those different places – whether they assimilated or
integrated or resisted acculturation in their interaction with the
host societies. It looked, too, at some of the views of emigration,
at some of the facts – and some of the myths.

Was emigration, is emigration a national haemorrhage, a
natural disaster, or a failure of politics or economics? Or did it
represent opportunity, challenge, the bugle in the blood?

Was the effect of emigration to spread Irish views and
interests? To contribute to the spread of Catholicism (if so, what
were the Scots-Irish doing) or to contribute as a yeast to the
culture of other countries?

And what of the effect in Ireland? Was emigration a safety
valve in the social system or a national social and economic loss?
Did the best go? Are they going now, the entrepreneurs, the
radicals, those who question and rebel? Leaving what?

Do those with get up and go get up and go? Do we export our
riches – or our problems?

And what of the emigrants – are they a national resource,
money in the bank for a developing Irish economy, a credit
balance of goodwill waiting to be drawn on?

What, too, of modern emigration – Is it quantitatively or
qualitatively different from the old (or what historic patterns of
emigration were perceived to be)? Are people drawn or are they
pushed? Do they represent the failure of an education system –
or its success?

What of movement to Europe? The wandering scholars could
move within a cultural universe stretching from Iar-Chonnacht
to Calabria and beyond. What will 1992 bring? Is movement
within a community, migration or emigration? Or, as Richard
Kearney argues 'is the widening of horizons within the European

Community predicated on a more intense focus on region and local community at home'?

Does modern travel and communication technology make a difference? If it is easier to get to Knock from Boston or Berlin than from Ballydehob, who then is the emigrant?

How permanent is emigration? Is it class differentiated? Who goes, who stays away, and for how long?

What does this mean for the society, for the economy, for education and other social policies?

The title of the 1989 Conference was Varieties of Irishness, borrowed in part from Roy Foster's lecture to the Cultural Traditions Group in Northern Ireland, funded as it was by the Ireland Funds. This could have represented a comfortable return to the womb of identity and certainty, but it was meant to be challenging, a challenge to cultural pluralism, to living together on this island, to self-examination and redefinition, to concern with communities, and to the meaning of Irishness in Ireland and elsewhere.

This was the thematic link with the 1988 conference in which many of the same people were concerned. Then the talk was of emigration, about the Irish diaspora both in historic and contemporary terms, but mainly about the Irish outside Ireland. That is, the Irish playing away. This, then, was the Irish playing at home. There were enough sportsmen in the audience to appreciate that home matches are often the more difficult and that more is expected of the side, that home crowds are fine when you are winning, but the first to criticise when things go badly. They love to bring their heroes down to size, they are the great deflators. The Irish are particularly good at this. There is an anti-hero culture that sits rather oddly with the glorification of dead heroes. Dr Johnson noticed this 250 years ago when he remarked 'The Irish are a fair people: they never speak well of each other.'· Perhaps we value the wrong things. As Bishop Philbin once wrote 'it's difficult to glorify a favourable trade balance'.

Why do the Irish appear to do so well abroad and not at home? Accepting for a moment that this is a huge generalisation based on rather dubious stereotypes, Why? What is the yardstick by which we measure success? Is there something in the culture which stifles initiative at home and which requires the physical and psychological release of exile or removal before enterprise can be released?

Above all, the discussion centred on people, especially young people, as Ireland's great national resource, and how the full potential of this could be tapped and released.

It talked, too, of the need for vision. The need for a strategic sense of purpose, the need to release energy in the society, imaginative and innovative energy that is there to be tapped, to celebrate excellence, to back the entrepreneur and the job creator, to recognise that people are the great resource and to release them from the shackles imposed by a centralised system of decision-making, by the education system, by the tax systems. How to develop them and enable them to develop enterprise. In Joe Lee's words, 'How to beat the begrudgers'. How to build on strength, how to reward endeavour and excellence. How to give people freedom to operate, to stimulate them to do so and reward them when they succeed. how to build on family and community. How to empower people to give them a true sense of responsibility and control, to replace dependence with true independence and self-confidence, how to draw on all the cultural and human resources of society, how to develop shared values and a culture which gives the cohesion and sense of direction that drives the whole thing forward.

Other speakers encouraged the people behind the Funds to use their business experience and contacts to help entrepreneurs in Ireland, to take a broader view of their individual and collective power and muscle and their ability to change situations. To think not only what can be done through the Funds – valuable, creative and seminal as that might be – but to think of practical contributions they might make from their own strengths, from their own experience and their own industrial and commercial activities.

The proceedings were enlivened, too, by the personal testimony of some of those who had received grants, by a vivid and moving presentation on community development in Derry by Paddy Doherty, on youth training in Londonderry by Glenn Barr, and by a moving exposition of reconciliation work in Enniskillen by Gerry Burns. These contributions, which greatly enriched the texture of the conference discussions, cannot easily be captured in the written word and are not reproduced here.

The conference finished on a note of hope and some

optimism, based on a perception of Ireland's youth as a national resource, forming a cohort of able, intelligent and concerned young people at a time when the European economy is producing a demand for such people and demographic trends in developed countries predict a shortage. The challenge to society in both parts of the island is to ensure that these young people can fulfil their promise and make their contribution – and that most of them can do so in Ireland.

All the speakers, in one way or another, paid tribute to the work of the Ireland Funds and to the inspiration of Tony O'Reilly as presiding genius. It was, for all of us, a particular pleasure to be associated with a philanthropic work which combines vision with practicality and which makes a significant contribution to building a sense of community in those areas where people face disadvantage and difficulty with courage and initiative. Seamus Heaney, in particular, described the Funds as 'having, as it were, applied the power of an international equipment to boost and transform the Irish vernacular'.

As he quoted the disclaimer of the mediaeval scribe who distanced himself from the magic of the message of which he was the humble translator, I close with its lineal descendant, the salutation of the seanchaí: 'Sin é mo scéal; má tá bréag ann, bíodh'. In other words, Don't shoot the messenger.

Correspondences: Emigrants & Inner Exiles

SEAMUS HEANEY

Ladies and Gentlemen,

'The keynote address' is a deeply pacifying phrase. It has all the steadying effect of words like *keel* and *anchor* and *bedrock*. It prepares you to feel reassured and confident. Which is all very well for you. But it has been a puzzle to me, as a person of literary interests, without even the barest rudiments of economics, without any worthwhile historical knowledge or political insight – it has been a puzzle to me to know what to say in a keynote address to a conference that is specifically geared to these very economic, historical and political matters.

Still, self-pity is never an edifying spectacle, and self-deprecation is always a suspect rhetorical move, so let me say right away that I intend to stick to the last. I intend, that is, to speak as a writer – which is to speak personally and exploratively, trying to come upon truth from traces of it inside oneself rather than from any evidence that might be adduced from the outside. Speaking as a writer involves following the sixth sense and proceeding on the off-chance; it involves testing the ground by throwing shapes; and, in general, it means advancing by the unpredictable path of intuition rather than the direct and earnest path of logic. For, as W. B. Yeats discovered (and liked to write in presentation copies of his books), 'Wisdom is a butterfly / And not a gloomy bird of prey'.

I am talking about a psychic event in which impulse discovers direction, potential discovers structure, and chance becomes intention. This is the movement I depend upon in all my other doings and writings, the only process that I trust, the only process that gives actions and statements an unshakeable psychic foundation. And I believe it is the same process which the Ireland Funds must be eager to identify in the multitude of projects which come to their attention and compete for their admirable, indispensable patronage. I want to argue, in other words, that creative work, whether it happens in the emergence of a lyric poem out of language or in the development of a community project out of local resources, creative work is like any other work. It involves moving a certain force through a certain distance. It involves the identification of an origin of energy, then the creation of conditions in which that energy can exercise itself freely in order to transform itself (and the conditions) into something new; and not just something new, but something actually renovated.

So what renovating thing can we say for ourselves this evening? What note can we key into? Renovation, after all, implies a certain amount of reliance upon the old resources and a certain reprise of the old motifs. 'We are earthworms of the earth', as one poet has said, 'And what has gone through us is what will be our trace'. Or, to express the same notion in a less enigmatic line from Yeats, 'What can I do but enumerate old themes?'

An old theme of my own, which is by no means original to me, is the doubleness of our focus in Ireland, our capacity to live in two places at the one time and in two times at the one place. That invigorating philosopher and prodigy, Richard Kearney, has claimed this to be a distinguishing mark of what he is bold to call 'the Irish mind', this capacity, shared by all traditions on the island, to acknowledge the claims of two contradicting truths at the one time, without having to reach for the guillotine in order to decide *either/or*, preferring instead the more generous and realistic approach of *both/and*.

No doubt this tendency has been strengthened by the need to acknowledge what Roy Foster has called 'varieties of Irishness'. At any rate, it still manifests itself in a multitude of ways, from the veteran's advice to young reporters in Belfast – 'If you're not confused, you don't understand the issues' – to my late mother-in-law's completely logical rebuke to one of her children who was taking more than her fair share of the cookies – 'If everybody takes two there won't be one each'.

We acknowledge the truth of this, even if we wish to escape

from something intellectually slippy at the centre of it. And that intellectual unease matches perfectly the social unease I felt when confronted with the doubleness of my own life twenty years ago in Belfast. I was in a fish-and-chip shop near Tate's Avenue, at a particularly tense moment in the politically disrupted life of that predominantly Protestant suburb. The night before I had taken part in a panel discussion on local television and the chip-shop assistant, a young woman of the English nation, had been watching the programme and recognized me. 'Oh,' she exclaimed, 'aren't you the Irish poet?' To which the proprietor of the shop, a lightly moustached and heftily corseted matron, true blue and scaresomely indigenous, cried out in reply, 'Not at all, dear. What's Irish about him? He's a British subject living in Ulster!' And then, victorious and impatient, she turned to me and added, 'Wouldn't it sicken you?' And I limply agreed. A classic case of *both/and*.

For as long as I can remember, therefore, I have been used to living in two places at the one time; and so have all the other people here from north of the border. To overstate that or to overinsist on it would be superfluous (and it could even be folksy). Living with contradictions is where it's at and where it is going to be, and already in Northern Ireland we are all veterans of that particular syndrome. As they say in Cork, yes too!

But south of the border there is also doubleness, a two-timing going on in the one place. The Republic may indeed be a country of conference hotels, computer printouts, fax and fish kills, property deals and stereophonic discos; but it is also, to a greater or lesser extent, the locus of an imagined Ireland, a mythologically grounded and emotionally contoured island that belongs in art time, in story time, in the continuous present of a common, unthinking memory-life. Only in Ireland, perhaps, could there have evolved a quasi-national holiday based upon a fictional character and dated to coincide with the art time of a work of pure imagination, set in Dublin on June 16, 1904. Twenty years later, and two years after the completion of *Ulysses*, Joyce wrote in his diary, 'Will anyone remember this day?' But he need not have worried. The national inclination to live by a time that is eternally recurring rather than chronologically hurrying past would stand him in good stead. Bloomsday is a modern manifestation of a way of being in the world that has been second nature to Irish people for centuries. 'We like to think', says Hugh O'Donnell, the schoolmaster in Brian Friel's play, *Translations*, 'that we dwell among truths immemorially posited'. The tone of Hugh's remarks may be ironical, but it is an irony to protect him from the collapse of his trust in the truth of the remark itself. Ireland, he senses, is about to fall out of time immemorial into historical time, out of custom into calculation, out of the once-upon-a-time into the time of timetables.

Evidence of such a transition from the one time system to the other happened to my wife and myself once, when we were on our way from Belfast to Waterford in the late 1960s. Suddenly we saw a signpost for Boolavogue, historically famous as the site of spontaneous local resistance during the rebellion of 1798. A song about the event commemorates Father Murphy spurring up the rocks with a warning cry and a rebel hand setting the heather blazing. Well, never mind the cruel addendum that rebel hands of the same sort had set the Protestants blazing in a barn at Scullabogue: the song had always been one of my mother's favourites, so there was a part of me that dwelt around that name immemorially posited in the Wexford landscape.

When I turned off the main road, therefore, it was to follow not so much a local bye-road as the route that Thomas the Rhymer took in the old English ballad; and in that ballad it was given its full Romantic title – the road to fairyland. I was driving not towards any civic or ecclesiastical entity called Boolavogue. I was rather driving towards the ever-receding centre of yearning in a musical cadence. I was following a signpost which brought me not so much into the geography of a parish as into the acoustic of a song.

At any rate, I had already gone more than the two miles indicated on the signpost when I met an old man on a bicycle. I pulled up and he slowed down. I screwed down my window and he screwed up his eyes. We gazed across the immense distances that intervened in the six inches or so between our faces. 'I'm looking for Boolavogue', I say, explaining myself, but also insinuating that in spite of my northern accent, there was nothing to fear about my particular variety of Irishness. 'Oh, you're past Boolavogue', he says. 'You'll have to turn and go back and keep your eye open for a church farther down on your right at the corner'. 'Oh,' says I, insinuating again, 'is that the church where

Father Murphy was?' 'Oh, it is', says he, 'but there's a different priest there now!'

It was a fine example of the entranced man being brought sharply down into the actual, a kind of farcical reprise of the Oisin motif; in a manner of speaking, I grew two hundred years old in a split second.

My illustration, however, is less important than the psychic phenomenon it is intended to illustrate, which is the doubleness we are capable of as inhabitants of time and place. And I want to go on to suggest that this two-tier world has a split-level language which is natural to it, and to us – a kind of unconscious bilingualism, an evolved verbal amphibiousness. Indeed, it would seem that there is a language proper to the eternal world that lies at the still previous point of our lives, and another language for the busy efficient world that occupies our hurried mornings, evenings and afternoons. Professor Proinsias MacCana has drawn attention to one delightful instance of these two languages, in his analysis of a famous scribal tailpiece which was appended to a twelfth century manuscript of the *Táin Bó Cuailgne*, and I shall come to that presently; but since we are all in Cork, it seems only fair to begin with a local example of the kind of phenomenon we are dealing with.

I am thinking about the story of the Cork schoolmaster who was certain that two of his pupils had been copying, but who was still uncertain as to which one of them was the copy*ist* and which the copyee. So one day he kept them in at lunchtime, set them together in a double desk at the back of the classroom, and gave them an essay to write about 'The Swallow'. As soon as they had both got started, however, he separated them to farther corners of the room, and when he collected the exercise books a few minutes later, he knew after only two sentences that he had the culprit. The whole incriminating and at the same time illuminating text read as follows: *The swallow is a migratory bird. He have a roundy head.*

When Professor John Cronin first told me this story, I realised it was a two sentence history of Anglo-Irish literature. First comes the correct, stilted schoolbook English, a kind of zombie speech which walks shakily out of the evacuated larynx where Irish once exercised itself with instinctive freedom. *The swallow is a migratory bird.* Then into this undead English there arrives the resurrected afterlife of the Irish and vigour is retrieved. The personality has found access to all its old reservoirs of sureness and impulse. Grammar goes wonky, vocabulary goes local, and an intelligence which had been out of its element in the first sentence gets right back into it in the second: *He have a roundy head*.

I cite this as another example of the Irish psyche flitting like a capable bat between the light of a practical idiom and the twilight of a remembered previous place, alert as any linguistic philosopher both to the arbitrariness of signs and the ache of the unspoken. And now, to extend the field of examples, I want to proceed to that twelfth century scribal tail-piece which I mentioned earlier.

At the conclusion of the long heroic narrative, *Táin Bó Cuailgne*, the scribe repeated in the Irish language (which was after all his mother tongue and the language of the epic itself) a formula which constituted the conventional conclusion to all such labours. It was a ritual invocation and it formally signified *The End*: 'A blessing on everyone who shall faithfully memorize *The Táin* as it is written and shall not add any other form to it'. Proinsias MacCana, writing about this passage in *The Irish Mind* (Ed. Richard Kearney), believes that the repetition of the words may have reminded the scribe of the story's ancient paganism, and that in compensation he then added the following codicil, which anxiously testifies to his Christian orthodoxy. Significantly, this affirmation of ideological correctness was written in pedantically formal Latin, and disclaimed all personal interest and responsibility. It went as follows:

> But I who have written this story, or rather this fable, give no credence to the various incidents related to it. For some things in it are the deception of demons, others poetic figments; some are probable, others improbable; while still others are intended for the delectation of foolish men.

Commenting on the difference of impulse, attitude and language discernible in these two scribal additions, Proinsias MacCana continues:

This nice example of medieval diglossia neatly epitomizes

the disparity between the cultural contexts of the two languages, Irish and Latin. On the one hand we have to do with a culture which is coeval with the Irish language and receives its only verbal expression through it, first orally and then from the late sixth century onwards both orally and in writing. It is a mythopoeic culture, innocent of secular chronology and locating people and events in a past by reference to genealogical filiation or to the reigns of famous kings, whether legendary or historical. On the other hand there is the Roman and international culture which was introduced to Ireland with Christianity and the Latin language and which extended its influence . . . from the first half of the sixth century onwards. It is the creation of a church rooted in finite time by the central fact of the incarnation and by its residual inheritance from imperial Rome, and in consequence it brought with it to Ireland a view of time and history, of secular and sacred, of artistic and religious categories that was radically at variance with that of native Irish society.

What MacCana is identifying as a rift in the twelfth century Irish consciousness has manifested itself in various ways ever since, and the most traumatically in the language shift from Irish to English. But that is a whole matter on its own, immense and inestimable in its consequences. More recently, however, over the past fifty years, it could be argued that the pattern which MacCana traces in his bilingual text matches very intriguingly the modern clash between an international style of commerce and culture and the more indigenous conservatism and traditionalism of Irish life generally. Corresponding to the Old Irish immersion in the phantasmagoria of myth, we have the demure, frugal, admirably visionary if intellectually obscurantist world of de Valera's Ireland – pastoral, pure and Papist; and corresponding to the organisational, ecclesiastical, administrative Latin culture, we have the rational, international, pragmatic spirit of Sean Lemass, Dr. Ken Whitaker and the First Economic Plan. Need I go on? Of course I need not.

The Latin disclaimer after the Irish blessing represents the same kind of disjunction and doubleness of value as that which we recognize when we hear of migratory birds and roundy heads, or hear the ghetto-blaster playing on the bog bank, or see the

Dallas architecture of Connemara bungalows. We acknowledge the historical inevitability of the thing but register that spiritual and aesthetic violence is being done. And yet it would be sentimental to expect the old world of season and custom and hallowed site and rite to have survived. Ten years ago, Liam de Paor pointed out in an article in *The Crane Bag* that even the best traditional musicians were now professionals. Indeed, it is futile to attempt to distinguish any more the categories of 'the traditional' and 'the commercial'. Aran sweaters are not for the people of Aran or even Ireland anymore. You associate Mayo with computers rather than caubeens.

The old world has been unfocused, literally. Indeed, this Latin word *focus*, meaning the hearth, provides us with a single, central, physical and etymological instance through which we can observe the big shift that moved Ireland from the old world into the new. This was a shift from the world of undifferentiated time and seasonal recurrence, settled values and absorbed rhythms, the world of ratified, common, impersonal modes of behaviour – a shift from that to the new world of individuated freedoms, economic independence, emotional self-direction, unsanctioned conduct and a secular, relativist permissiveness. In this new world, the very word *hearth* sounds like an anachronism. In fact, those who are old enough to remember the actual closing of open hearths in country kitchens and their replacement by bandy-legged iron stoves, and then the removal of the stoves and the indiscriminate positioning of radiators round the walls – those who remember this have already inscribed in the memory-bank of their bodies a record of the almost physical consequences which one's being suffered in the process of modernization.

The hearth had indeed been the focus, the centre, the heat and the heart of the house's meaning. Any hearth was all the hearths there had ever been. Every morning the fact of fire was wonderful all over again as the primal flame was gratefully rekindled. Fast forward then, as they say in the video business, to the central heating system, and abruptly you have the cancellation of wonder. Your being is insulated from the physical and metaphysical life of flame. Your space has been made abstract by an imposed grid of pipe and radiator. You have comfort but you also have something inside you that is out of alignment. In a dumb old part of yourself you have left the world of roundy heads and entered the world of migratory birds. You are stumbling about in the international Latin and suppressing the hearth Irish. You are a secular, modern citizen of the world with a sort of lacuna in your midriff. You are capable, comfortable and a little displaced. You are vaguely in exile from somewhere inside or outside yourself, but you don't quite know how or why. You are probably a professional, urban, Irish eighties success story. You may even be London Irish, or American Irish, or Canadian Irish, but whoever you are, you feel this vestigial capacity to focus around an old field of force that is neither marked on the map nor written into the schedule.

And then, by accident, you get back to some ancient familiar location, somewhere with a sort of pre-natal purchase on you. An old house say, like the one I found myself in recently, where I lifted a latch for the first time in years; and there, in that instantly cold metal touch, in the pleasing slackness and scissor-and-slap of the latch mechanism, something unpredictably invigorating happened. My body awakened in its very capillaries to innumerable and unnameable rivulets of affection and energy. The moment that latch made its harsh old noise, a whole ancestral world came flooding up. And that inundation persuades me that in all of us (the lacuna in the midriff notwithstanding) there is a supply of dammed-up energy waiting to be released.

In other words, a connection is possible between your present self and your intuited previousness, between your inchoate dailiness and your imagined identity. Your Irishness, to put it in yet another way, constitutes a big unconscious voltage and all it needs is some transformer to make it current in a new and significant and renovative way.

I am now proceeding, as I promised I would, by intuition and indirection, on the wing of metaphor and suggestion. But I still believe I am proceeding towards the kind of truth we would want to key into, for it seems we have here an analogy for the emotional structure of a modern, creative, patriotic action. A correspondence could be posited between the unsatisfied and unspecified excitements that my latch set off in me, and the sharp desire that all of us occasionally experience to pay into an effort that would have renovative effects upon the unfocused yet beloved Ireland of the present, North and South.

And just as one can find an energy source in the ghostlife of a lifting latch, so one can base an intellectual and philanthropical project upon fidelity to some absent but intuited Ireland of the affections and the imagination.

Please understand therefore that all my talk of bog banks and latches and hearths and visits to Boolavogue, and all my relish of folk speech in Cork and loyal speech in Belfast are not sighs for a lost Ireland. They are not, I hope, simply the usual cry, 'God, but aren't we a great ould crowd'. Rather, I intend them as little points of recognition and I want to suggest that it is upon exactly such chancy manifestations of affection and connection that we must build a work of meaning.

Creative work, as I said in the beginning, is a matter of impulse discovering direction, of potential discovering structure, of chance becoming design. What is exemplary about the members of the Ireland Funds and the work they do is the way they have combined their impulse to drive off the main road and enter the acoustic of the song world with their capacity to find Boolavogue by the exercise of modern technological navigational aids. The Ireland Fund and, before it, the American Irish Foundation successfully found ways of allowing their members simultaneously to live in dream time and to keep abreast of the historical moment.

I know, from long association with many of you, that your impulse is ancestral, local and at times blessedly whimsical. But I also know and applaud the fact that your impulse does not just exist at the usual level of self-gratification. On the contrary, you have made that impulse exercise itself and transform itself (and the Irish conditions) into something renovated. You have applied, as it were, the enabling power of your international equipment to boost and transform the operations of the Irish vernacular.

Still, if self-deprecation is no way to begin a key-note address, flattery may be a tactless way to end it. Much as I would like to pour the oil of eloquence upon the greatly deserving heroic head of A. J. F. O'Reilly and play the bard to his Ard Rí, I will leave you instead with some lines by T. S. Eliot, lines which encompass chastely and beautifully much of what I have been stumbling crookedly in pursuit of. They apply to the purposes and functions of the Ireland Funds generally; and they also apply to all emigrants and inner-exiles, of whatever variety of Irishness. They come from T. S. Eliot's *Four Quartets*, from the section called 'Little Gidding' and they address with classic succinctness the core of the matter which I too have been considering. Let us call it, finally, the use of memory:

'This is the use of memory;
For liberation – not less of love but expanding
Of love beyond desire, and so liberation
From the future as well as the past. Thus, love of a country
Begins as attachment to our own field of action
And comes to find that action of little importance
Though never indifferent. History may be servitude,
History may be freedom. See, now they vanish,
The faces and places, with the self which, as it could, loved them,
To become renewed, transfigured, in another pattern.'

Emigration: A Contemporary Perspective
J. J. LEE

The resumption of emigration from the Irish Republic in the 1980s, when about 200,000 people left – about 150,000 of them in the second half of the decade – came as a shock, and to many as a disappointment, after the net immigration during the 1970s had seemed to signal a historic reversal of the migration trends that had persisted for several generations.[1] Insofar as the ending of emigration had been a frequently claimed objective of the struggle for independence, the continuation of emigration after independence, and particularly the exodus of the 1950s, when emigration reached its highest rate since the 1880s, induced a demoralising sense of failure among those who took the potential of sovereignty seriously. The sharp reduction in emigration during the 1960s, when the rate fell to one third that of the 1950s, and the change from emigration to immigration in the 1970s, were hailed as marking a watershed in the performance of the independent State. It was therefore all the more disconcerting, given the intense emotions inspired by the issue, deriving from the fact that the emigration figures were often used as a rough proxy for national success or failure, when the trend shifted abruptly in the eighties. Debate resumed once more on the causes and consequences of emigration.

The debate on emigration stretched back to the eighteenth century, and assumed particular intensity when a million people fled the country as a result of the great famine in the mid-nineteenth century. Three phases can perhaps be loosely distinguished in the debate since then.

The first phase lasted from the Famine itself to roughly 1900. During this phase, nationalists were instinctively inclined to blame the continued loss of the 'bone and sinew' of the country on alleged landlord exploitation and British misrule. Once the

33

land question was effectively settled in the 1880s, however, and the burden of landlordism lifted from the farmers' backs, the situation became more complex. Irish society was now evolving a self-image of a spiritual, morally superior haven of virtue in a world dangerously threatened by English materialism. It became increasingly difficult to explain the continued flight of its own people from the holy island. In addition, a fairly comfortable urban and rural middle class was now busy adding the ha'pence to the pence. Life could indeed be comfortable for those in a position to consolidate their comforts in early twentieth-century Ireland. The ultimate beneficiaries of the Famine and of the land settlement had to become more selective in their interpretation of emigration. The British, of course, remained until 1922, but a civil Irish society had already emerged. Some organs of middle-class opinion therefore began to shift the emphasis from emigration as the consequence of imperialist tyranny to emigration as an index of the psychological inadequacy of the emigrants themselves. The *Freeman's Journal*, representative of the Home Rule Party, lamented that

Irish girls, beguiled by hopes of fantastic wages abroad, give up more than they know, when instead of the simple neighbourly village life, or the friendly relations still existing in good Irish households, they choose at a distance the tawdry, uncertain splendours of a despised servant class, and take on themselves the terrible risk of utter failure far away from all home help. It is surely true that scarcely one Irish girl abroad is ever happy again at heart.[2]

The blame could now be laid on the inadequacy of the female character rather than on any aspect of the society itself. Fortunately for this point of view, women accounted for slightly more than half of total emigrants – in striking contrast to the situation in continental Europe where women constituted about one third of the total. After independence, some held that the impact of Hollywood, projecting images of lavish and romantic American lifestyles, further unbalanced already flighty female minds, seduced by fantastic visions of the luxury awaiting them. Even after the Second World War, there were commentators who insisted that emigrants to Britain were deluded because the real standard of living of the Irish in London was lower than it would have been had they had the wit to remain at home.[3] The Director of the Central Statistics Office would stress in 1951 that 'it is a gross over-simplification to suggest that emigration is due solely, or even principally, to lack of economic development in Ireland'.[4]

Common to these observations was an assumption that the lack of employment, and the consequent lack of marriage opportunities, which left the Irish by 1950 with the highest proportion of bachelors and spinsters in any country in Western Europe, was not a decisive factor for either male or female emigration. This view was probably not widely shared at popular level, but it seems to have appealed to many policy-makers and advisors. It is understandable why this should be so, however much individual motivation must remain a matter for conjecture. The assumption that emigration was due mainly to non-economic factors could serve a useful function. It relieved economic policy-makers of responsibility for solving the problem. If emigration was mainly the result of 'obscure, traditional, psychological factors', as a Department of External Affairs memorandum suggested in 1947,[5] then there was little anybody could do to induce the emigrants to remain at home.

There had always, of course, been politicians and officials who refused to share this view. They did not achieve ascendancy, however, until the late 1950s. As emigration soared during that sad decade, it became more difficult to sustain the inherited degree of complacency, although some succeeded in reassuring themselves that everything was still for the best.[6] But T. K. Whitaker, appointed Secretary of the Department of Finance in 1956, and Seán Lemass, who became Taoiseach in 1959, both believed the fundamental problem to be economic. Since then, in what may be considered the third phase in the debate, the economic interpretation has held sway, although most would accept that some emigration is due to simple boredom. However, the decline of emigration in the 1960s and 1970s corresponded with improved economic prospects, and its resumption in the 1980s coincided closely with economic stagnation. It now seems accepted, both by the official mind and by leading economists, that the main causes are indeed economic.[7]

If so, should or can anything be done about the problem? Is it even a problem any more? Perhaps the most celebrated comment of the 1980s on the whole issue was that made by the Tánaiste (Deputy Prime Minister) and Minister for Foreign Affairs, Brian Lenihan, who told *Newsweek* in October 1987 that emigration 'is not a defeat because the more Irish emigrants hone their skills and talents in another environment, the more they develop a work ethic in a country like Germany or the US, the better it can be applied in Ireland when they return. After all, we can't all live on a small island'. This observation deserves attention for several reasons. Although Mr. Lenihan has been not unknown to affect a style of amiable vacuity at home, he is both a highly intelligent man and an experienced politician, having served as Minister for Justice, Education and Agriculture, as well as for Foreign Affairs. He is a deservedly popular figure, who can be presumed to be in touch with the grass roots. It is unlikely that his views do not reflect widespread feelings. How compelling, then, are the assumptions underlying the belief that 'we cannot all live on a small island?'.

'All' now amounts to 3.5 million of us in the Republic. Is this the maximum, or rather more than the maximum, population that the country can sustain at its present standard of living? If so, it means that the optimum population density for Ireland is about 50 per square kilometre. How does this compare with the rest of the EC? It transpires that far from being densely populated, Ireland is the most sparsely populated EC country. One might not expect it to compare with the notoriously densely populated Low Countries. The Netherlands has eight times the population density of Ireland, Belgium more than six times. But even the less densely populated EC countries still have far higher population per square kilometre than Ireland – West Germany five times, Italy nearly four times, Luxembourg nearly three times, Denmark, France and Portugal, double, even mountainy Spain and Greece, 50% more. This does not necessarily mean that Ireland is under-populated. There may be specific reasons why she could not support a larger population at a rising standard of living. But it is not easy to think of what they are. Denmark supports double the population density with no natural resources. Spain has overtaken us recently in terms of income per head despite her rain-starved soil and her barren plateau.

Perhaps the problem lies in our being 'a small island'? Perhaps there is something in the nature of 'islands' which condemns them to lower population densities than continental states. Even a cursory glance at island populations casts doubt on this assumption. Strictly speaking, of course, the Irish Republic is not an island. It has a land frontier! But let us assume, for argument's sake, that it is an island and that Northern Ireland is a second Irish island. It transpires that Northern Ireland has about double the population density of the Republic. Whatever the problems that unfortunate entity has to cope with, over-population is not normally counted among them. Britain has a population density more than four times higher than the Republic. Japan has a density more than six times higher. There are, of course, more sparsely populated islands, like New Zealand. But there seems to be no law decreeing that islands cannot sustain populations as dense as those of mainlands. The unfortunate suspicion therefore arises that, if there be a key word in Mr. Lenihan's formula, it must be 'we'. This is a far cry from the hopes of little more than half a century ago, when Eamon de Valera and Seán Lemass, like many earlier nationalists, liked to contemplate a population soaring to twenty million or even more. Such fertile fancies clearly failed to take account of economic realities at the time. Nevertheless, it is Ireland which appears the odd man out in European population history. Every EC country has significantly increased its population this century, even if many of them now have very low birth rates. Economists might have considered the Netherlands already grossly over-populated in 1919, when it had a population density of about 200. Yet it has more than doubled its population since then, from 6.8 million to 14.6 million in 1986, while simultaneously increasing its standard of living faster than Ireland. There seems, in other words, to be a positive rather than negative correlation between population growth and economic growth in twentieth-century Western European history. Indeed, the most rapid population growth in European history, from the mid-eighteenth century to the third quarter of the twentieth century, coincided with the longest period of sustained economic growth. Historians are still trying to disentangle the complex relationship between the two, but Malthusian type fears that 'we cannot all live in this small Europe' have not yet been realised.

None of this means that Ireland may not constitute a legitimate special case. But it does rather shift the onus of proof onto those who claim that Ireland is already over-populated. There can be little dispute that emigration is a good thing for the majority of emigrants. They themselves, and even more their children, who might never have been born had their parents remained in Ireland, have generally prospered abroad. Although particular groups may suffer relative hardship at times – like some of the illegals in the USA at present – there can be little question about the balance of individual advantage. The real question is whether shorter term individual advantage chances to coincide with the longer-term national interest. Any answer to that question must remain to some extent subjective, depending as it does on varying, and sometimes conflicting, perceptions of what constitutes national interest. Alexis Fitzgerald, for instance, son-in-law of Taoiseach John A. Costello and advisor to Garret FitzGerald, eloquently expressed the view in his reservation to the *Reports of the Commission on Emigration* that emigration operated as an important safety valve which helped preserve the stability of Irish society and the values associated with that stability.

I cannot accept either the view that a higher rate of emigration is necessarily a sign of national decline or that policy should be over-anxiously framed to reduce it. It is clear that in the history of the Church, the role of Irish emigrants has been significant. If the historical operation of emigration has been providential, Providence may in the future have a similar vocation for the nation. In the order of values, it seems more important to preserve and improve the quality of Irish life and thereby the purity of that message which our people have communicated to the world than it is to reduce the number of Irish emigrants. While there is a danger of complacency, I believe that there should be a more realistic appreciation of the advantages of emigration. High emigration, granted a population excess, releases social tensions which would otherwise explode and makes possible a stability of manners and customs which would otherwise be the subject of radical change. It is a national advantage that it is easy for emigrants to establish their lives in other parts of the world, not merely from the point of view of the Irish society they leave behind, but from the point of view of the individuals concerned whose horizon of opportunity is widened . . . while we should so cultivate our resources that as many Irishmen as possible can live their lives in Ireland this should not be done in a manner or to the extent of imperilling the imponderable values and liberties of our traditional society. I cannot look forward as to an improved state of society to an Ireland where a greatly increased population can be supported only at the expense of a reduced standard of living.[8]

This analysis begs many questions.[9] Many would doubtless agree with some of the sentiments expressed. For our present purposes, however, the passage requires decoding. What it meant in practice was that emigration reduced potential threats to the existing distribution of property and income, or to existing educational opportunities for those who could afford them. In the terminology made familiar by Albert Hirschman, the 'exit' of the emigrants conveniently eliminated the danger that if they remained at home they might give 'voice' to their presumed resentment. Emigration took the pressure off, and contributed to a quiet life for the more comfortable classes. There was little doubt that it was a good thing for those sectors of Irish society who enjoyed security and prosperity. But the national interest cannot be wholly equated with making Ireland safe for the possessing classes. Those classes produced some remarkably able representatives in the professions, in the legal, medical and ecclesiastical worlds. What they signally failed to produce was entrepreneurial talent in the narrower economic sense. Indeed, even today, in view of our dependence on foreign investment for three-quarters of our industrial exports, Ireland would seem to have the weakest indigenous entrepreneurial class in capitalist Europe.

It is impossible to arrive at any remotely 'scientific' conclusion about the impact of emigration unless we have some idea of what our optimum population might be. That estimate in turn depends on so many assumptions that a whole range of plausible figures could be suggested. The economists have provided few clues as to how we should approach the question. Perhaps they are wise, given the pitfalls involved. Professor Brendan Walsh, an outstanding Irish authority on demography, is one of the few to have ventured an opinion.[10] Walsh concludes that 'if there had been no net outflow since 1840, we would now have something like four times our present population . . . I tend to the view that if restriction of emigration opportunities during the 19th and 20th centuries had caused our population to rise to fourteen million, Ireland would now be a poorer and uglier country than the one we know today'.[11] That is certainly a tenable viewpoint, probably one which would command widespread assent. His reasons are, however, instructive:

> The possible adverse effects of rapid population growth on our standard of living should not be underestimated in the light of our very poor record of generating employment at an acceptable standard of living over the last two centuries. Furthermore, we should not dismiss the effect of a higher population density on the quality of life in this country in the light of our poor record of environmental management, despite having the lowest population density in Europe'.[12]

It is difficult to argue with this view. Certainly, if the Irish did not improve their economic and environmental performance then a population of fourteen million would be a disaster. Walsh does concede that

> It is, however, fair to say that the emigration option has allowed Irish people to avoid the harsh discipline that has laid the foundations of prosperity in countries with few natural resources and high population density. In this sense, emigration has offered a 'soft' option, both for those who leave and those who remain behind.'[13]

His conclusion from this, 'however, we should be slow to criticise people for accepting a soft option, when it is available'! does rather beg the question. 'Those who leave' usually have little choice. Society has failed them. But 'those who remain behind' are in a different category. They have responsibility for the condition of the country. If they decide to 'accept a soft option' it says little for their concept of collective responsibility, or for that vaunted value system which Alexis

Fitzgerald so cherished.

Walsh is sceptical about the argument, sometimes advanced, that

> in the absence of the possibility of large-scale emigration the pressure of rapid population growth combined with the benefits of retaining the brightest and best of each generation in the country, would have transformed the Irish economy and society. According to this view, we would have been forced to become a north-western European version of the Dutch or the Taiwanese.[14]

As he notes, it is impossible to find evidence in support of this hypothesis, simply because it didn't happen. The evidence he cites against it, consisting of consequences of very short-term increases in population, can hardly be considered decisive. We do know that fear of a return wave of emigrants after the Second World War spread something like panic in the Irish government, even to the extent of setting up an Economic Planning Committee in 1942 to try to devise full employment policies. As soon as the threat of a return of the emigrants receded, the Committee fizzled out.[15] For what it is worth, only naked fear could jolt an Irish government into thinking of emigration as an emergency, as distinct from a way of life, at least until the Lemass-Whitaker era.

Two further comments may be made on the Walsh argument. We do not require to become 'a north-western European version of the Dutch or the Taiwanese'. To sustain a population of fourteen million we need 'to become a north-western European version of' the Italians! Fourteen million would give us a population density approximating that of Italy, not that of the Netherlands. If national stereotypes have any validity, that should be a less daunting challenge!

The second point worth noting about the Walsh scenario is that fourteen million is not the only alternative to 3.5 (Walsh does not advance it as such. He chooses this figure because it is a plausible estimate of what population would now be had there been no emigration. My concern here is with the optimum population starting from now rather than from 1850). It may well be that there is some figure, or range of figures, between 3.5 and

14 million that would serve the national interest better as we approach the twenty-first century. A population of seven million would probably still seem extraordinarily big to most Irish people. Yet it would raise our population density only to the level of Northern Ireland. It is when we begin looking at what constitutes normalcy elsewhere that we begin to realise that there is nothing inherently implausible about scenarios of a bigger Irish population. Indeed, if the current Irish population situation did not exist, postulating it would itself seem inherently implausible, so wildly does it deviate from any western European 'normalcy'. The implications of a population density equal to that of Northern Ireland for economic activity in the Republic – for the size of the home market, the effective utilisation of infra-structure etc. – have not been explored. It doubtless seems a waste of time to do so at present. But no serious discussion of optimum population size can be conducted in the absence of such estimates. Economists are therefore likely to operate on thought processes very similar to that of the rest of us in this field – on hunches, instincts, guess work. Almost as striking as the extraordinary population experience of Ireland is the extent to which economists, with only a handful of honourable exceptions, have chosen to treat that population experience as if it were virtually an external factor parachuted into the society, instead of being the most fundamental expression of the society's values and aspirations.

It is churlish to continue to pick bones with one of the few economists to seriously ponder the emigration issue, particularly when he makes so many shrewd points, like the nonsense of a capital importing country investing in the capital intensive education of graduates for export.[16] But one may raise a last query. Professor Walsh, no doubt correctly, attributes much of the emigration of the 1980s to the economic policies of the 1970s, which resulted, through bad judgement compounded by bad luck, in the slump of the eighties, which chanced to coincide with an unusually high rate of entry into the labour market. He does not therefore see it as the consequence of 'a lack of collective will "to do something" to prevent it'.[17] This can be accepted with respect to the abrupt changes of the late 1980s. But it should not divert attention from the longer term issue of the priority to be given to employment in framing national policy. It has been argued, notably by Therborn, that one reason why small European economies including Sweden, Norway, Finland, Austria and Switzerland, succeeded in keeping unemployment below 5% when it was rising to double digit levels in several other European countries, was their commitment to full employment policy, however varying the techniques they adopted.[18] Needless to say, full employment cannot be conjured up simply by employment policy. Sometimes no policy at all would have yielded better results than the policies actually adopted. But if the first prerequisite for an employment policy is intelligence, the second is political will, precisely that 'collective will' to accord the creation of sustainable employment a high national priority. To what extent that will really exists in Ireland must remain a matter for debate. If emigration diden't exist at present, it would be necessary to invent it to keep unemployment figures from soaring well over 20%.

It is better than nothing that the Irish government, prodded by concerned citizens and particularly by the Catholic Church, which pioneered its own welfare services for emigrants in London in the 1950s, now accepts some minimal responsibility for assisting the emigrants adjust to life abroad, at least to the extent of making small donations to various organisations that concern themselves with emigrant welfare.[19]

The emigrants most in need of these services are likely to be found at the weaker end of the emigrant scale, rather than the type Mr. Lenihan and others envisage, moving with assurance and self-confidence from one country to another, honing their skills and developing their work ethic before returning to Ireland. How many of the latter type there actually are, only time will tell. It is not very clear why they should want to return to Ireland if they are successful abroad. Perhaps it will be the less successful ones who return? Or, if we are all Europeans now, why should we in Ireland be bothered if they ever return, at least as long as they stay in Europe? Is that not their home just as much as Ireland? And are they not really internal migrants, and not emigrants at all, in this brave new European world? Such a scenario has already been postulated by some public figures. Is this perhaps the best hope for Ireland? – or is it yet one more example of the tension between individual and national interest, one more variation of the inherited capacity for self-delusion as yet another generation of Irish equip themselves to evade responsibility for the quality of national performance?

Footnotes

1. For estimates of emigration figures for the 1970s and 1980s see T. Corcoran, 'Tracking Emigration Flows' in Joe Mulholland and Dermot Keogh (eds.) *Emigration, Employment and Enterprise* (Cork and Dublin 1989) pp. 30, 32 and 'Emigration: An Official Perspective' in *ibid*, p. 91. This whole volume provides an exceptionally useful survey of the current situation.
2. *Freeman's Journal*, 24 February 1908.
3. *Irish Press*, 2 January 1948.
4. R. C. Geary, 'Irish Economic Development since the Treaty', *Studies*, 40 (December 1951), p. 402.
5. SPO, External Affairs memo, 30 August 1947.
6. 'Favourable Aspects of the Irish Economy' *Irish Banking Review* (December 1958), pp. 8-9. For a wider range of reference on the issues considered here, see J. J. Lee, *Ireland 1912-1985: Politics and Society* (Cambridge, 1989), pp. 373-86.
7. See for example, Brendan Walsh, 'Emigration: An Economist's Perspective' in Mulholland and Keogh (eds.), *Emigration*, pp. 17-19, and 'Emigration to the United States – an official perspective', *ibid*, p. 89.
8. A. Fitzgerald, 'Reservation No. 2', *Reports of the Commission on Emigration and other problems* (Dublin 1956), p. 222.
9. For a critique, see Lee, *Ireland*, pp. 381-4.
10. See his contributions in Mulholland and Keogh (eds.), *Emigration* and 'Emigration: Some Policy Issues', *Irish Banking Review* (Summer 1989), pp. 3-14.
11. Walsh, 'Emigration' in Mulholland and Keogh (eds.), *Emigration*, p. 25.
12. *Ibid*.
13. *Ibid*, p. 26.
14. *Ibid*, pp. 25-6.
15. *Lee, Ireland*, pp. 226-32.
16. Walsh, 'Emigration', in Mulholland & Keogh, p. 27.
17. *Ibid*, p. 19.
18. G. Therborn, *Why some people are more unemployed than others*, (London, 1986). See also the succinct treatment of the issue in K. Kennedy, 'Ireland and European Integration – An Economic Perspective', in Dermot Keogh (ed.), *Ireland and the Challenge of European Integration* (Cork and Dublin, 1989), pp. 35-40.
19. See Bishop Eamonn Casey, 'Emigration: The Reality – The Church's Response', in Mulholland and Keogh (eds.), *Emigration*, pp. 34-35; Bobby Gilmore, 'Emigration Begins Before You Climb on the Boat', *ibid*, pp. 46-51, and 'Emigration to the United States – An Official Perspective', *ibid*, pp. 97-8.

Irish Emigration to Britain Since World War II

LIAM RYAN, Maynooth College

The past one hundred and fifty years have witnessed the greatest mass migration of human beings in world history. Vast populations have been uprooted by war and famine; equally vast numbers have voluntarily left their homeland in search of a cure to what the modern sociologist is apt to call downward social mobility. Whether pushed or pulled from their native land, this century and the last have seen great streams of humanity on the move. These have included peasants in search of new jobs, emigrants in pursuit of new worlds, and refugees fleeing from old worlds of hunger, persecution and genocide. By the late twentieth century, however, in most western nations this process had come to an end. In Ireland alone does emigration persist with a nineteenth century intensity. In Ireland alone in 1988, probably unique among the nations of the earth, did the number leaving the State (45,000 approx.) come close to the annual number being born (54,000).

Emigration is at the centre of the Irish experience of being modern. It has been the safety valve that has enabled Ireland to cope successfully with the problems of transition from a traditional rural society to a modern industrial one. The transition has been made possible by the simple expedient of Ireland offering a modern way of life to 75% of its population. The remaining 25% have had, for a long time past, a choice of unemployment at home or migration abroad; they have always generously chosen to promote the welfare of the 75% at home by opting for the latter alternative. Consequently, to discuss Irish emigration in the twentieth century is virtually the same as to discuss Ireland, since there is scarcely a single political, social, economic, intellectual or religious problem which has not been

45

influenced directly or indirectly by emigration. Emigration is a mirror in which the Irish nation can always see its true face.

The Irish are a people peculiarly disposed to emigration, so much so that it is sometimes easier to explain why they wander rather than remain at home. Certainly, for all our assertions of patriotic love of country, we have repeatedly proven that, given free access to any country with a standard of living higher than our own, we will readily relocate. While mass migration of the nineteenth century was largely to America, that of the twentieth century was largely to Britain. The attraction of America was tangible and irresistible – the land of opportunity, good wages, enticing descriptions returning in every envelope, often accompanied by solid evidence in the form of passage money. Migration to Britain never had the glamour of migration to the new world. Yet the shorter distances involved, together with the many social and cultural ties between the two islands have made large-scale to-and-fro movements inevitable. Indeed, an Irishman arriving in the South-East of England might have seemed no different from the Welshman, the Yorkshireman or the Scotsman were it not for the fact that the Irish have always had that uncomfortable habit, common to most foreigners, of being Catholic. Then too there was the added political or colonial dimension. An entire history of migratory links between Britain and her former colonies was well captured in the slogan of protesting Commonwealth immigrants whose banner some years ago proclaimed: 'We Are Over Here Because You Were Over There'.

Between 1976 and 1981, well over 100,000 emigrants returned to live in Ireland, the vast majority from Britain. However, as is well known, this reversal of the pattern of over two hundred years was shortlived and by the mid-1980s the annual number leaving Ireland had again reached the peak levels of the 1950s. It is estimated that some 45,000 have emigrated in each of the last three years, that over 70% of these have gone to Britain, and that the majority have settled in the London area.

Over the past one hundred years, the number of Irish emigrants to Britain has been well over two million. The only figures available are for net migration which do not include those who subsequently returned to Ireland. It is estimated that since 1900 two out of every three Irish emigrants settled in Britain.

Table 1: Net Migration from Ireland (26 Counties) 1881-1976

10 Year Periods	Total Number
1881-1891	597,325
1891-1901	396,414
1901-1911	261,539
1911-1926	405,029
1926-1936	166,751
1936-1946	187,111
1946-1956	316,331
1956-1966	292,608
1966-1976	43,000

(Source: Census Reports)

Throughout the early twentieth century, the number of Irish-born in Britain grew steadily, reaching a peak of almost one million in the 1960s. There is an obvious decline throughout the century in the percentage of emigrants opting for Scotland. In 1901, the Irish-born in Scotland constituted 32% of all Irish emigrants in Britain; by 1971 this had fallen to just 5%. Indeed, as the century progressed, Irish emigrants tended to show a marked preference for the South-East of England and for London in particular.

Table 2: Irish-born (26 Counties) in Britain in Relation to Total Population

Census Year	England & Wales	Scotland
1901	426,565 (1.3%)	205,064 (4.6%)
1911	375,325 (1.0%)	174,715 (3.7%)
1921	364,747 (1.0%)	159,020 (3.3%)
1931	381,089 (0.9%)	124,296 (2.6%)
1951	627,021 (1.4%)	89,007 (1.7%)
1961	870,445 (1.8%)	80,528 (1.6%)
1966	878,530 (1.9%)	69,790 (1.4%)
1971	685,620 (1.3%)	35,365 (0.7%)
1981	579,833 (1.2%)	27,018 (0.5%)

(Source: Census Reports)

The stereotyped emigrant was single, young, unskilled, with just primary education, arriving off the boat-train to English cities with little money, no job and nowhere to live. Undoubtedly, many did fit the stereotype but there were also the middle-class migrants armed with a Leaving Certificate or a university degree, with a fair knowledge of where they were going and what their expectations were. Characteristically, both types were interested only in short-term gains since they assumed that they would stay only a few years and then return home. The ability to delude oneself that emigration was temporary has been one of the most persistent features of Irish migration to Britain among all social classes.

Like most emigrants, the Irish tended to concentrate in Britain's urban centres. If we take 1971 as a typical year, over a quarter of the Irish lived in London where they constituted 3.8% or 1 in 26 of the total population. The remainder were concentrated in cities such as Manchester, Coventry, Birmingham and Liverpool. The following Table, derived from the Census of Population, gives a regional distribution of Irish-born in Britain in 1971 when the Irish community was at its peak.

Table 3: Regional Distribution of Irish-born (26 Counties) in England & Wales 1971.

Region	Number Irish-born	As % of Pop.
Southeast	359,250	2.1%
North West	95,830	1.4%
West Midlands	91,975	1.8%
Yorkshire/Humberside	34,300	0.7%
East Midlands	31,565	0.9%
South West	29,065	0.8%
Wales	14,220	0.5%
North	10,010	0.3%
East Anglia	9,655	0.6%

Census records are, of course, an inadequate measure of the size of the Irish community. They only record the numbers of those whose birthplace is Ireland. Children of immigrants, however Irish their characteristics, are consequently excluded, as are all those who marry into the Irish community. The first great wave of Irish migration to Britain came to an end with World War I. The tide had been mounting since the last quarter of the eighteenth century, but had dwindled to a trickle by the 1890s. Emigration to America, however, remained at a high level with an average of 60,000 annually until 1914. The gradual closing of the open door to America led to a turning of emigrants eastwards towards Britain during the 1920s and 1930s, and in the decades after World War II this produced the second great wave of Irish migration to Britain. The Census of 1966 saw the largest number of Irish-born ever recorded in England and Wales. It is to an examination of that community that we now turn our attention.

Why They Went: Push-Pull Factors
Irish twentieth century emigration is an extremely complex phenomenon and the assumption that it is due mainly to economic causes requires some qualification. While not all migration was rural in origin, a sufficiently high percentage was to warrant beginning our analysis there. And while rural Ireland has changed enormously in the past thirty years, what has not changed is that the land of Ireland does not provide an adequate living for those who depend upon it. As a result, the relationship of people to land in Ireland has always been one of conflict rather than one of affection. One of the problems has always been that the majority of the farms of Ireland can support only one family at a time. And even then the typical family was a good place to bring up children only to about the age of fifteen. Children were reared in reasonable comfort, with a good diet, with love and affection, and in a sufficiently attractive environment, but as to what their future was after they left school – generally at fourteen – there was absolute silence in the home, in the school and in the wider community. It was a standard Irish solution to a problem – if one ignored it, it might go away. In the end, it was often the children rather than the problem that went away. Today, there is much more discussion and openness, and if children do migrate they do so responsibly with their parents' blessing rather than exiting furtively as many did forty years ago.

In the past, an exchange of hints in both directions – including veiled suggestions of emigration – became a substitute for real communication. There was, however, one type of family in rural

Ireland for which the phrase 'I might go to England' was a real and genuine threat. The social class consciousness of the day quickly divided the neighbourhood into families that emigrated and families that did not. There were, of course, parts of Ireland where emigration was a reality for every family, but in much of Munster and Leinster a real class division grew around emigration. To the unskilled and unemployed and farm labourers, England seemed a land of opportunity, but to the fifty acre farmers and to the petty bourgeoisie of the towns and villages it seemed like a kind of ghetto for Irish people, a kind of vast Irish slum where none of the better people went, not even on holidays. And the threat of a son or daughter taking the boat-train was a threat that the family name might be tainted with the mark of the emigrant and coupled with the labourers and others who somehow weren't good enough to get work at home.

Often, due to the great silence and sheer inertia of rural Ireland, the second factor in emigration began to operate – the pull of those already away. Emigration to Britain was often the result of a sudden impulse. A week's wages would pay the way over, and if things did not work out, another week's wages would pay the way home again. A letter from a friend, contact with relatives, the travellers' tales of holidaying emigrants, any of these might trigger the individual act of migration, but the stage had been set long before. The annual influx for holidays of men with money in their pockets who could impress their peers in the local pub, and their families, with the newly-found phenomenon of the self-drive car: these from the early 1950s onwards opened up a whole new horizon to the dwellers of rural Ireland. It enabled both locals and emigrants to recapture briefly the companionship and gaiety of a youthful Ireland. It often brought home to the locals that the comradeship and the laughter, no longer in the community, may indeed have migrated to Britain along with their friends. And so the crowd which came on holidays always went back augmented. This had very little to do with emigration as the sociologists understand it. It was more the continuation of a social relationship which was maintained rather than lost by migration. These were not dreamy young men and women lured by bright lights and distant cities, but rather lonely people who followed their own kind wherever they may be – it just happened that they were in English cities.

This process was especially operative in the Gaelic speaking districts like Connemara, which developed an in-word to describe it which soon was of general use. It was the word 'Crack', a word which sometimes in its early use caused embarrassed laughs when used by an outsider, almost as if a family word had been discovered by a non-member. For the Connemara man, the word 'Crack' was a magical word which connoted all that was pleasurable in human society. More especially, it meant the jovial company of one's own people. Basic to it was the belief that one's own can provide one with the greatest pleasure, for indeed there was no higher pleasure than 'good crack'. And so many of them left Ireland simply because 'the crack was over there', in Camden Town and Cricklewood, in the Irish communities, Irish dancehalls and Irish pubs of London. It was not the freedom and excitement of big city living that constituted the pull factor. Indeed, when the rural emigrant returned to Ireland on holidays his conversation was never about the advantages of city life, but about the adventures and achievements of the Irish community. To listen to a typical group of returned emigrants in an Irish pub one would imagine that only Irish people existed 'over there', almost as if the native Londoners had gone away and handed the city over to them.

Not everyone, of course, found what they were looking for. Many escaped from the loneliness of the Irish countryside into a loneliness of their own in England. Others merely exchanged one type of alienation for another because even when they found good work and good money, they were after all in a foreign land, among foreign people who at best were indifferent and apathetic when not openly hostile. In Ireland, they had thought of England primarily in terms of their own people, those who had such a good time and such display of wealth during summer visits. In England, they thought of Ireland primarily in terms of their own place, where they really belonged, and where one day they might yet realise their ambitions. While in Ireland, they had idealized life in England, and now in England they tended to idealize the situation back home – images and memories of laughing crowds and sunny evenings – only to return and find in the words of so many emigrants that 'it was a different place altogether'. And so, having collected further images and impressions that only make them miserable, they long for

England again or long for Ireland as it once was before they ever saw England – always memories, dreams and myths, but never quite able to accept reality in either country.

In so many ways, James Joyce was an archetype of the twentieth century Irish emigrant: physically separated from Ireland but obsessed with it; unable to live there but unable to live without it; alienated from its religion but in dress almost a priest-like figure in sombre clothing, haunted by ritual, Latin phrases and scholastic philosophy; spending most of his adult life abroad, yet could write of nothing but his own Irish microcosm, a city he was wont to describe as a place of paralysis.

Adjustment, Acculturation and Prejudice
The Irish, like migrants everywhere, went where they had relatives, but even with the help of friends, arrival in a strange land can be a traumatic experience. It demands an immediate process of orientation, finding one's way about, the grind of looking for a job or for somewhere to live, an elaborate maze of relocation and, above all, of interpretation. For the newcomer, there is always much that is unfamiliar – uniforms, accents, attitudes, signs – even quite simple things can produce substantial shock and profound perplexity. In the case of many an Irish emigrant arriving in Britain, the basic problems of migration were compounded with sheer irresponsibility. The man who wouldn't dream of going to Dublin without a job and a place to stay often stepped readily off the train at Paddington or Euston with no skills, no jobs, no contacts, no money and nowhere to live.

Throughout much of this century, there was a complete lack of any organised effort to help the migrant to adjust to life in a new society. The few that came into existence in the 1950s, the Irish Centres, were largely sponsored by the Catholic Church in Ireland, were totally inadequate to deal with an influx of 50,000 people annually, but in impossible circumstances succeeded in helping many. The Irish Government, fearful of the political consequences of appearing to encourage emigration, did nothing at all to help the migrants in Britain and even less to prepare them while in Ireland by disseminating knowledge of society in Britain, its opportunities and its problems. Nor did it make any effort to protect its child emigrants and other immature members of the community from the serious and often life-time damaging effects of their own irresponsibility. For over fifty years the Irish Government continued to deny that it had any responsibility in the matter until, at last, some sanity began to prevail in the early 1970s. The British Government created no special organisations or groups to deal with the massive problem, but simply channelled Irish immigrants through the everyday processing machines of employment exchanges, welfare agencies, and social security offices.

A job and a roof over one's head have always been the immediate needs of migrants. They have also been the two main areas of competition and possible conflict between immigrants and the native population. As far back as 1821, Southey was voicing the fears of British workers that Irish peasants would 'shortly fill up every vacuum created in England and Scotland, and reduce the labouring classes to a uniform degree of degradation and misery'. In the post-war years, however, when labour shortage was acute in Britain, the Government went to considerable expense to settle in Britain those displaced in Europe by the war. Polish soldiers and their dependants constituted the largest single group, but altogether some 457,000 European migrants entered Britain in the 1946-50 period. It was with these rather than with the native workers that Irish immigrants had to compete. Indeed, there was little competition because the rebuilding of Britain called for more workers than were available. The chronic shortage of unskilled labour created a market almost tailor-made for Irish immigrants, men who had lived by muscle and strength and a few simple tools. The development of the motorways in the 1950s and 1960s continued the demand for this type of worker until the increasing mechanisation and sophistication of the construction industry of the 1970s made their particular contribution – tons of brawn and ounces of brain – redundant.

The majority of Irish men found their way into the construction industry where their hard-working, hard-drinking habits created not merely the enduring image of the typical Irish migrant, but also the myth of the big money and the big spenders back in Ireland. A sizeable proportion of Irish workers, especially those from Irish cities, were attracted by factory employment, but there are no myths at all concerning Irish factory workers in Britain. They tended to become part of that rather cosmopolitan complex of industrial labour where one integrates quickly into the work pattern and learns how to utilise all the advantages of the system – trade unions, insurance policies, eligibility for council housing etc.

For Irish girls, the task of securing employment was not very difficult in the post-war period, and like their men-folk many were satisfied to begin work in jobs which native labour was no longer willing to accept – domestic work, waitresses, factory employees, chamber maids. On the other hand, the relatively high numbers entering nursing and office employment meant that Irish girls never had quite the same working-class image in Britain as their men-folk acquired. For Irish girls, the problems were never quite as acute as for men. Many of them were recruited while still at home – as high as 65% in the case of nurses – and came to Britain with a job and accommodation already arranged. Many too began in live-in jobs such as domestics or in hotels and hospitals. There was always good hostel accommodation for girls who were prepared to pay a little extra, and many a secretarial Irish girl began there and used the hostel as a springboard from which to find a flat. The hostel too provided ready-made social contacts and became almost a continuation of boarding-school experience – only now they went to work and not to school.

Reading the literature on Irish migration, one could easily be forgiven for thinking that only men emigrated to Britain. In fact, women have always been as numerous as men in the migration statistics and, from the mid-1950s onward, outnumbered them in choosing Britain as a destination. Yet this unusual emigration pattern has gone largely unnoticed and the range of these women's lives remains unexplored. Recently, a book *Across The Water* by Mary Lennon and others has done something to redress the balance. It contains a unique collection of oral testimonies which effectively challenge stereotypical notions of the Irish by examining the unrecognized experiences of women migrants and by exploring what the authors call 'the resounding silence waiting to be filled'.

Negative stereotypes of the Irish have traditionally abounded in Britain and though now somewhat dated are still trotted out by the tabloid press whenever the occasion demands, such as

IRA bomb attacks in Britain. Although the offensive housing and employment advertisements have long disappeared, some discrimination still occurs even if it does not have the intensity of anti-new-commonwealth prejudice. Some Irish emigrants are likely to mistake English indifference for hostility, yet at some time or another almost everyone will have met with some rudeness or insolence. A native wishing to hurt or insult can always pick on the difference in a migrant – accent, eating habits, colour or faith. In angry or irrational argument the Irish may get called 'bloody Micks' or 'bog-Irish' or 'a bunch of Paddies', but in Britain there never has been a really rude word for the Irish. If the British do have a fault, it is their inability to take the Irish or Ireland seriously, and this has often caused friction and resentment.

The average English person tends to have a stage-Irish perception of the migrant, and irrespective of what level of society one entered, from labourer to lecturer, one was likely to be confronted with little jibes from the English delivered in a good humoured way about the fact that one was Irish. Instead of treating this as a bit of fun, many Irish, because of an inferiority complex about England and the English, tended to see it as a continuation of seven hundred years of persecution. Generally, the mind of the average emigrant was so full of myth and mist, of prejudices and warnings, that he never quite knew how to react to the reality he found across the Irish Sea. A large disabling factor was often their lack of confidence in their own Irishness, and sometimes afraid that they would condemn themselves the moment they opened their mouths, they resorted to telling lies and using false names as a defence mechanism. This became particularly operative when faced with the inevitable task of form filling. The Irish man or girl brought with them all the native cunning, all the petty prejudices and simple virtues of an island people, and that included a basic dislike of surrendering information to strangers. They did not understand the process, and they distrusted what they did not understand. Their education had not been sufficiently broad to make them realise the value of surrendering certain types of information, and it took them some time before they were willing to accept that people were trying to help them and not trap them.

The Pub and the Paddy

There were many reasons why twentieth century Irish-born in Britain began to build their social life around pubs, but the most important was that it was the one place where they could find the warm, relaxed atmosphere that becomes a substitute for home. There was the alternative of the Irish dance-halls which indeed always exhibited an enviable gaiety; they were always very lively and very Irish, but one needed these same qualities in one's heart and in one's feet to find them inviting. They tended to be dominated by a younger set recently arrived from Ireland, and those past thirty did not usually find them an attractive place to spend an evening. Virtually the only other places for Irish people to meet were the Irish clubs. Some were attached to particular churches, or particular counties, or linked to sports groups like the GAA. Whatever their origins, their ability to become focal points for Irish migrants was limited by the fact that they had an added moral purpose of not just entertaining the Irish but of unifying them or educating them or protecting them or helping along some great cause or other. In short, if you wanted to meet Irish people, have a casual good time with no strings attached, then you went to the pub and not to the club.

London's pubs were classified by the Irishman as Irish pubs and the rest, and generally speaking he did not go to the rest. In the Irish pub he was surrounded by other Irishmen, the talk was good and the crack was good, and there was a reversion to a completely Irish way of life. This was all the more enjoyable because the average migrant was conscious of the ways he differed from the British and had a certain inferiority about exhibiting these cultural traits in public, but with the help of a few beers and the support of fellow-travellers he quickly put that behind him. In addition, Irish pubs were where old friends back in town could congregate, and as they became centres of music and gradually ceased to be all male establishments, they were one of the few places where Irish men could meet Irish girls; in short, a place to meet both old friends and new.

For those who had neither, the Irish pub also held out the prospect of employment and living accommodation. At very worst an Irishman looking for a bed for the night would always find someone who would let him sleep on the floor if nothing better were available. But above all else, the Irish pubs were the labour exchanges for the building sites. They were the places where a man looking for a job was always sure to meet someone who knew someone, and certain foremen from certain sites were known to frequent certain pubs, and there was always the chance of a favourable introduction.

In 1966, 38% of all Irish-born males in Britain were in the building industry. British Labour Force Surveys of 1985 and 1986 show that the percentage twenty years later is still close to 33%, three times greater than the rate for the remainder of the white population. In London especially, the Irish dominated the industry from top contractors such as Murphy, Fitzpatrick, and McInerney, through the sub-contractor level where hundreds of Irish operated the 'lump' system, to the vast army of the unskilled Irish who represented the twentieth century equivalent of the labourer at all ages – the men who built the Pyramids or the great medieval cathedrals, the eighteenth century canals or nineteenth century railroads. Construction work was particularly attractive to the Irish migrant, partly because it offered plenty of money, partly because it was unskilled, with lots of overtime, and partly because the peasant mind saw in it the industrial equivalent of ownership of land – independence, relying on one's health and strength, tied to no employer, no contract, no trade union, free from tax officials and insurance agents, each man for himself in a tough world.

To the British they became known as the 'Paddies', a word used more in description than in derision and, indeed, one taken over by the workers themselves, who were often proud of the 'Paddy' image they conveyed. They tended to glorify feats of hard work and hard drinking, and took pride in the fact that these had been immortalised in ballads such as 'McAlpine's Fusiliers' or 'Murphy's Volunteers'. Indeed, the military parallel of many of these songs was quite apt because Irish building labourers had many of the characteristics of an army: a uniform of old clothes held together with big leather belts, heavy nail boots, the distinctive walk of men who looked as if they were perpetually plodding across ploughed fields, a distinctive stance that was neither a slouch nor fully upright, a weaponry of picks and shovels, and never-ending lines of lorries for transportation. Early morning parade was at collection points like the tube station at Camden Town from where they were whipped away in lorries into the darkness. In the evening, they reappeared like men back from battle but still in battalion formation, always in a group, which is why they were the most visible and distinctive section of the Irish in Britain. Even on Sundays, their parade uniform of blue suits and brylcreemed hair had about it the hallmark of collective identity.

Everything about them was distinctive, especially their work attitudes. They had nothing but scorn for restrictive trade unionism, they had little pride in skill, but considerable pride in the ability to work long and hard, particularly in bad conditions. They constantly boasted of feats of hard work they had achieved or had seen others achieve. To have one's name mentioned around the pubs in connection with a feat of this kind was to have achieved the very pinnacle of fame. Such feats of hard work were, of course, functional for the employer and for Britain too, but in a different way, they were functional for the worker as well. The ability to work hard was an assurance of independence, and it was assumed that only a bad worker would stay tied to one employer. There was sometimes loyalty to a foreman, but never to an employer. To be 'owned' by an employer, to be known as a 'Murphy man' or a 'Wimpey man' or a 'McAlpine man' was equivalent to being called a poor worker in a world where no man stayed long enough to call any man his boss.

Despite the constant affirmations that 'it was every man for himself in this game', they worked in groups, lived in groups, drank in groups, almost as if life were a burden that could be lessened in proportion to the number of shoulders that bore it. Despite all the bravado, many of them were lonely men without families or homes, or much expectation from life. They sometimes complained of the parasitic locals back in Ireland who 'shake your hand, clap your back, drink your drink, call your name, but know they've found a fool', or an individual burdened by his conscience might in a state of semi-intoxication disclose 'what a lousy bastard I am, I don't even write to my mother'. On such occasions when they did give some insight into their inner world, amid the memories, the guilt, and the incoherent wisdom, one often found a warmness and a tenderness that belied some of the savagery of the world in which they moved, a world in which there was little respect for the weak and respect for the strong only while he remained so. That same attitude of mind meant that they never faced the English community as equals. They faced it only as conquerors, either at the level of the big contractor who had conquered London and could face a British firm in complete self-confidence, or at the level of the labourer where one constantly heard stories of 'this English bloke who said . . . but we showed him' or tales of 'this other bloke who thought he was tough but when we put him to the test . . . .'

The whole combination of circumstances which created the world of the 'Paddy' began to change dramatically in the mid-1970s. For one thing, the Irish themselves began to change. The responsibility of a wife and family and the security offered by national insurance had persuaded many building workers to work regular hours at regular pay. With the exception of the Channel Tunnel construction, which has brought back the labour camp and the huge money, the rest of the industry has become more like the work patterns of industrial employment. In the long run, it was the worker rather than the Inland Revenue which suffered most from the 'lump' system. The constant danger of accidents, of unemployment, of tax evasion, coupled with a declining demand for unskilled labour, a more vigorous trade union invasion of the industry, and a general economic recession, have all produced a more rationalised construction industry and a more settled and enlightened Irishman as well.

Integration and Upward Mobility
At a St. Patrick's Day dinner in 1966, Donough O'Malley, then Minister for Health, told the National University of Ireland Club in London that they should play a fuller part in the political and social life of Britain. Irish emigrants, he said, must recognize that they cannot be citizens of Britain and Ireland simul-taneously. Nostalgic sentimentality about the old country should be rejected. The Irish did not exert an influence on British polit-ical and social life commensurate with their numbers, and he suspected that it was partly due to a fear of betraying their Irish heritage. At the time there was considerable controversy about his advice, but no controversy about his initial assumption that the Irish had not integrated well in Britain. In fact, Irish assimila-tion into British society is among the fastest that occurs among

immigrant groups anywhere in the world. Assimilation is practically complete in a single generation. The children of Irish immigrants, sometimes to the distress of their parents, grow up seeing themselves as English or Scottish; they may acknowledge their Irish ancestry and exhibit a few inherited traits, but for all practical purposes they are indistinguishable from their British peers whether in speech or dress or in social, cultural or religious behaviour.

However, back in the mid-1960s, the Irish did seem to many observers to be gravitating towards cultural ghettoes with a proliferation of Irish clubs and pubs, dance-halls and associations. Twenty years later it is evident that these centres of Irish interest have not been obstacles to integration, precisely because they were used as stepping-stones to the larger society. In the initial years of migration, in their efforts to survive the storm of transition from one society to another, the Irish temporarily anchored themselves to what was known and familiar, but the majority were well able to weigh anchor once the storm had passed.

In the early post-war years, conscious of the stereotyped image of the Irish as unruly and irresponsible, the reaction of the middle-class Irish was: 'we are not all like that; what about our doctors, dentists, lawyers and bankers; if only we could make these more visible perhaps the Irish image would improve'. The reaction was entirely in terms of 'we' and 'they', and of showing 'them' that 'we' had not all come from the bog still speaking and looking like those quaint comical characters of some Victorian melodrama. The emphasis was on image, not so much the integration of an elite as the identification of an elite. The Irish in the gutter had dragged the whole ethnic group down with them, and this could be remedied not by reaching into the gutter to uplift those who may have been there but by capturing alive some sober respectable specimens of Irish birth and putting them on display in a stately Belgravia mansion. In this way, the Irish Club in London was born in 1951. It became a centre to which the Irish middle-classes could bring their English friends, the sort of place to which British politicians came to reveal in St. Patrick's Day speeches that they had Irish ancestry.

Much has changed since the Irish Club was at its peak in the late 1960s. Nowadays, image is not so important. The New

Commonwealth influx has taken the emphasis off the Irish and there is, in any event, no longer the same monocultural demand that immigrants change their traditional ways and conform to conventional British standards. British society is today much more heterogeneous than it was. For instance, a 1989 study of the Inner London Education Authority showed that 70,000 youngsters in ILEA schools spoke as many as 184 different languages. In this situation, differences are expected and tolerated, and the Irish are accepted for what they are – different human beings, who like all immigrants may be expected to do things differently.

For the first time it became possible in 1971 to estimate from the Census Tables the actual number of Irish-born people in various occupations. In that year there were in Britain: 4,000 Irish-born doctors or dentists; 31,000 nurses; 3,000 industrial engineers and scientists; 2,300 civil engineers and architects; 3,600 clergymen; about 1,800 journalists, actors and artists; and some 10,000 teachers of whom close to 1,000 were in universities, polytechnics or colleges of education. When we consider that in that same year there were in Ireland itself a total of 3,500 doctors and 19,000 nurses the full extent of the brain-drain from Ireland becomes evident. The greatest concentration of fully integrated Irish born in Britain is probably to be found in the medical profession. Generally, Irish doctors have a good standing in Britain, especially with their patients, and while the higher social classes would probably prefer not to have an Irish doctor, the same is not true of the working classes. Nursing is also a profession in which the Irish-born also integrated quickly and in which they have made a significant contribution. It was also a profession in which they had a high rate of advancement. In the mid-1960s, for example, when Irish-born constituted 12% of total nursing staff, they also constituted 11% of senior nursing staff in England and Wales.

The election to the House of Commons in 1969 of Irish-born Michael O'Halloran encouraged an increased involvement of the Irish in British politics. In many ways, O'Halloran was typical of the newly integrated Irishman – a man of modest formal education, a clerk in the building industry, retaining an unmistakeable Irish accent after twenty years in England, and owing his election neither to an Irish vote (only 8% of the constituency) nor to advocacy of Irish issues, but rather to long-standing service with Islington Council and long association with the Labour Party. In the subsequent local elections of 1971, over 150 Irish-born candidates presented themselves to the electorate, 100 more than at the previous election. The majority of these stood for Labour – some 75%. Six Irish-born candidates were elected to Islington Council, another six to Luton Council, and three Irish-born were elected mayors of British cities, Derby, Luton and Kettering. Although this level of success was not maintained in subsequent elections, it did herald a new and significant participation by Irish-born in post-war British politics.

Generally, an Irish person's progression towards an appreciation and an acceptance of British society comes in the order of appreciating people, then systems and institutions, and finally values. The surrender of one's Irish heritage follows a similar order, criticism of people leading to a critical questioning of institutions, leading to doubts about basic values. This is particularly true of religion where criticism of Irish practices always begins with the priest, then passes to a questioning of the Church and doubts about ultimate values. However, the universal character of the Catholic Church is sufficient to preserve a basic religious identity which paradoxically might be less strong were it seen by the emigrant as a purely Irish institution. The contribution of Irish Catholics to the English Church has been very significant, even if it has been largely numerical. Without the Irish-born, the Catholic Church in Britain would be a singularly truncated church, proud of its survival, perhaps even fascinating liturgically and intellectually, but too much of a minority to be of consequence. Irish immigrants have at least served to make Catholicism in Britain a religion of the poor as well of the rich, of the city rather than of the countryside, and of the present rather than of the past.

One of the best indicators of integration is the rate of inter-marriage between the immigrant and native populations. Data for England and Wales became first available in 1970 and showed a very high rate of Irish/British inter-marriage.

The figures in Table 4 show that almost one half of Irish-born had married a spouse not born in Ireland. The vast majority of these had married British partners. In fact, in only 36% of marriages did both partners come from Ireland. This is particularly significant in view of the fact that the large number of Irish immigrants favoured endogamous unions as did the fact that the Irish were one of the few ethnic groups not having an excess of males. It demonstrates that even by 1970 theories of the social and cultural ghetto were largely myths.

And Problems Not A Few
Considerable attention has been paid to the 'success' or 'failure' of the Irish in Britain. It has been the aspect of emigration that in the post-war decades continued to fascinate the Irish at home. Stories of those who had found gold on the streets of London were paralleled by tales of Irish vagrants and prostitutes on those same streets, and returning emigrants found themselves constantly queried by natives curious to discover the latest gossip about their acquaintances. Interest in the Irish in England seemed at times to be really interest in the sins of the Irish in England. Occasional statistics on crime, delinquency, vagrancy, unmarried mothers, prostitution, lapsing from the faith, all received prominent attention in Irish newspapers, and there was growing alarm about the social and moral dangers inherent in the emigrant experience.

Clearly, the very composition of the Irish emigrant grouping made them prone to a high appearance in the social problem

Table 4: Intermarriage Rate.
Data for Marriages in England and Wales 1970

Place of Origin of Spouse	Irish-born Males	Irish-born Females	Total Irish-born
Ireland	11,783 (52%)	11,783 (54%)	23,566 (53%)
Great Britain	10,229 (46%)	9,176 (42%)	19,405 (44%)
India & Pakistan	50 (.2%)	178 (.8%)	228 (.5%)
New Commonwealth	84 (.8%)	373 (1.6%)	457 (1%)
Australasia/Canada	38 (.2%)	25 (.1%)	63 (.1%)
Other Foreign-born	255 (1%)	336 (1.5%)	591 (1.3%)
Not Stated	51 (.3%)	97 (.4%)	148 (.3%)
TOTAL	22,490 (100%)	21,968 (100%)	44,485 (100%)

Source: Registrar General's Statistical Review of England & Wales, 1970)

statistics. Along with those who came to Britain seeking a better life, there came also the misfits, the psychologically disturbed and the criminal. Ireland tended to export her problems with her people, and the combination of inadequate personalities coupled with inadequate preparation meant that a persistent stream of irresponsible Irish people were constantly appearing before employers, landladies, welfare officers, and inevitably before magistrates, prison warders and probation officers. Irresponsible emigration took many forms. There were the men who had been given the promise of a job over a few pints in an Irish pub during the summer and who found to their dismay on arrival in London that their benefactor had changed lodgings and left no address. Many a penniless wife and young children came following a will-o-the-wisp husband to similar non-existent addresses. Most pathetic of all were the inadequate personalities who came looking for the 'geographical cure', something almost endemic in the Irish emigrant situation, the belief that problems can be solved or fortunes can be made simply by moving. For those with serious problems, of course, the geographical cure did not work because their faults were in themselves and they soon discovered that each fresh move was only a fresh mistake. If they had failed under the relatively favourable circumstances of home life in Ireland, they were most unlikely to succeed under the most unfavourable circumstances of a vast anonymous metropolis.

Research throughout the 1950s and 1960s continued to show that in proportion to their numbers in the population, Irish people were over-represented in the numbers of people with social problems. The prison statistics of the period demonstrate well the magnitude and the persistence of just one of the many problems.

The Irish-born statistics are those from the Republic of Ireland only. The problem is seen in perspective when we consider that throughout the 1960s the average annual intake into prisons in Ireland was about 1,800 and that the daily average number in prison in Ireland scarcely ever exceeded 400 in the decade. Taking the 1969 British statistics, predictably enough Irish men account for 37% of all sentences for vagrancy and 29% of all drunkenness; Irish women account for 22% and 15% of all sentences for drunkenness and prostitution respectively.

Table 5: Receptions into English & Welsh Prisons, 1960-69

Year	Sex	Irish-born Receptions	Total Receptions	Irish-born as % of Total
1960	M	2,926	40,514	7.2%
	F	158	2,418	6.4%
1961	M	3,271	44,057	7.4%
	F	230	2,561	9.0%
1962	M	3,703	50,612	7.3%
	F	85	2,832	3.0%
1963	M	3,568	51,813	6.9%
	F	100	2,765	3.6%
1964	M	2,924	51,257	5.7%
	F	125	2,514	5.0%
1965	M	4,392	54,230	8.1%
	F	182	2,284	8.0%
1966	M	4,667	59,943	7.8%
	F	110	2,583	4.3%
1967	M	4,490	58,643	7.7%
	F	214	2,342	9.1%
1968	M	3,502	47,650	7.3%
	F	126	1,608	7.8%
1969	M	3,713	53,159	7.0%
	F	146	1,665	8.8%

(Source: Personal Communication from the Home Office, London)

An explanation for the high crime rate can be offered in terms of the disproportionately high numbers of Irish immigrants in the crime-prone group: single men aged 18-30, with poor education and low socio-economic status. The Irish too have always been over-represented among the urban poor and among the residents of decaying city areas where crime is high.

More importantly, while the Irish are over-represented in the statistics of social problems, they have always been under-represented in the numbers of staff employed to deal with these problems in the various statutory and voluntary agencies in Britain. Aware of this, and conscious of the fact that London was rapidly becoming a city littered with bits of Irish humanity, the Catholic Church in Ireland undertook a major programme of help. Special chaplains were sent to work in England with the migrants, social centres were established in the major cities to provide practical help, special employment agencies and housing associations were set up, and social workers were organised to meet the immigrants almost as soon as they got off the train. The evident need for these organisations declined in the late 1970s as the numbers migrating dwindled. A decade later, however, with an estimated 3,000 problem immigrants per annum seeking help from Irish centres and agencies in London, it is business as usual.

And What of the Irish at Home?
The ambivalence always displayed towards emigration in Ireland itself is well illustrated in some of the 'comments' of the official *Commission on Emigration Report* of 1954: demographically, it has reduced the population and increased the burden of the aged; politically, it has given Ireland 'a significance abroad that is out of proportion to the size of the home population'; theologically 'it has helped the cause of Christianity in many countries'; psychologically, it may have weakened 'national pride and confidence' and thus retarded 'the efforts required for national progress'; economically, it has made possible a higher standard of living both for those at home and those who left'; morally, some emigrants may have succumbed 'to the temptations of city life'; and while this 'moral and religious deterioration' is not extensive, it is however 'sufficient to be disturbing'.

In a free, independent Ireland, emigration had tended to be the barometer by which the success or failure of the nation was judged. It consequently demanded explanation, especially from the three dominant groups who had largely been responsible for fashioning that nation – political nationalism, the Catholic Church, and the middle-classes both farmers and townsmen. Unable or unwilling to accept that the Ireland they had created was itself part of the problem, they resorted, as Kerby Miller has shown, to the defence mechanism of traditional categories of thought which enabled them to interpret twentieth century emigration in comforting customary ways.

The first of these was the interpretation of emigration as exile, as a fate suffered by the nation, something collectively imposed from outside. The 'curse of emigration' motif, emigration as a communal necessity, relieved both political and clerical leaders of any responsibility in the matter, especially as they preferred to live with the myth that Ireland's ideal and unchanging social order could in time support all its people. In the meantime, however, Ireland must remain rural because the solution of industrialization and urbanization would itself generate more problems than it would resolve.

On this basis, churchmen and politicians could condemn both emigration and the emigrants themselves. Mass departures abroad somehow constituted a weakening of the ranks, and emigration to England was especially seen as opting for the materialistic and secular way of life. Emigration was always from sinless Ireland to sinful England, so the emigrants went away abundantly blessed but insufficiently prepared by parents, priests or politicians who tried to compensate for their inadequacies by sending them on their way with not merely the ten commandments but with five hundred other commandments as well. For many emigrants, of course, the warnings and the dangers only served to make England appear more attractive. But it had a darker side as well. As seen from Ireland, there might well be big money in England, but somehow that too was tainted by the sins of England, and if an emigrant returned with money earned on the building sites of London to buy a farm or a pub, he often found himself spurned by the local middle-class as if his hands and his money were not as clean as theirs.

The sinless Ireland/sinful England comparison was really an extension of the romantic view that cities are evil places, and country villages are good places. It was also part of the inability to see England or the English in realistic terms. But above all else there was the inability to see the emigrants realistically. A standard of behaviour was expected of them that was far in excess of anything demanded at home. They were blamed for what they did not do in Ireland, and for what they did do in Britain; they were expected to acquit themselves as successful citizens wherever they went, and at the same time not give up their primary loyalty to Ireland; they were expected to raise exemplary families in Britain, and at the same time to sustain their family of origin by subsidising the Irish farm from the English factory. They were indeed expected to achieve a great deal, and the fact that so many succeeded has been an achievement worthy of a considerable people.

Of Three Minds

DR. GEORGE QUIGLEY

"It was said of the great literary figure and controversialist, G. K. Chesterton, that he was not sufficiently dull to be authoritative. Joe and Richard have combined wit *and* authority.

Can our 3-pronged session achieve coherence? At the end of it you may wish to apply to yourselves some lines of the American poet Wallace Stevens:

> 'I was of three minds,
> Like a tree
> In which there are three blackbirds.'

Rather than comment in detail on what has been said so far this morning, I propose to offer some reflections from a Northern perspective, stimulated by statements in two well-known texts from the pens of both speakers."

In his pamphlet 'Myth and Motherland'[1] Richard Kearney wrote that, without mythology, our hopes and memories are homeless. But he also warned about the dangers of myth if totally divorced from the challenge of reality. Joe Lee, in 'Whither Ireland?'[2] emphasised the need to forge the type of mentality essential to sustain long term collective achievement and foster a 'commitment to consensus rather than conflict'.

If I were seeking to subsume those texts in one sentence, I would use the words in which the great French writer Anatole France defined a nation: 'A nation', he wrote, 'is a communion of memories and hopes'. Another Frenchman, Ernest Renan, entered a caveat. He said that the essence of a nation is that all who comprise it should have much in common and should have forgotten much. But is forgetfulness really an option – say in Ireland, where our consciousness of history serves as the very instrument to preserve and sustain the identity and loyalty of communities?

And if there are difficulties with memories, what about hopes, when the aspirations of different communities appear so irreconcilably divergent?

Perhaps it would help if there were a more general recognition that 'a nation's life begins where its politics leave off'. Those are the words of Thomas Kettle, an ardent Irish nationalist who died in the Battle of the Somme in 1916.[3] They leave no room for obsessional politics. They envisage a society where politics invigorates but does not monopolize life.

But realism bids us also recognise that politics is the medium within which questions of power are usually worked out. We can, however, avoid the illusion that the issues can be *finally* settled. That illusion was passionately rejected by Kettle. Describing his own hopes for Ireland he wrote: 'Freedom is a battle and a march. It has many bivouacs but no barracks'. To put it more generally, politics is as often about pursuing a *process* as about achieving a *condition*. The American philosopher John Dewey put the same point in rather different terms. Truth, he wrote, can be bought only by the adventure of experiment.

This implies that, in politics, there are few problems to which there are 'correct' solutions discoverable by pure thought. Solutions are the product of social interaction, of what is akin to a market in ideas. Politicians offer what are in effect products – packages of values and measures which enable people to express their priorities and combine their preferences. And we should bear in mind that the essence of a true market is the promotion of reciprocity.

Viewed in this way, politics is the testing of a range of hypotheses about public policy. The outcomes are determined by the ability of the participants to make and keep bargains. It is not a matter of hit and run but a process of give and take, in which we are not only driven by the spur of our aspirations but constrained by our limitations.[4]

How important is it for the kind of approach which I describe that there should be a nexus of relationships which constitute genuine community? Is there room for cultural pluralism?

I would suggest that we can learn a good deal about the needs of society by examining how modern writers on management are viewing companies and other organisations. The message of two of the most famous of them – Peters and Waterman – is that the excellent companies are both centralized and decentralized or (in their phrase) loose-tight. Purpose and stability in the organisation are achieved not by rigidly prescriptive rules but by the existence of a few transcending values covering core purposes. It is in the companies in which culture is dominant that the highest levels of true autonomy occur. The culture regulates rigorously the few variables that count. Core beliefs provide stability in a changing world. They create a sense of pride. Shared values are merely one of 7 attributes of the successful company which Peters and Waterman built alliteratively around the letter S. Some, like structures, systems and strategies, constituted the hard 'S's'. Others – shared values, staff, skills (or capabilities) and symbolic behaviour (or style) – constituted the soft 'S's'.[5]

Transferring this to the context of society in general, I would argue that we need to give attention not just to institutional arrangements but to culture and style. In society as in companies, the 'Vision' document is as necessary as the annual budget and may, indeed, be the essential means of achieving it.

What roles do History, Tradition and Myth play in identifying shared values and generating Vision? Socrates said that the cohesion of society is dissolved when the same events delight some and dismay others. 'The best run state' he said 'is the one in which as many people as possible use the words "mine" and "not mine" in the same sense of the same things.'[6] History, Tradition and Myth have not contributed to that end in Ireland.

First, History
Much of what passed for the writing of history was, it has been said, a compound of cliché and hackneyed error. The past was a malleable thing in which one could find whatever one was hoping for in an ideal future.[7] The outstanding work done by historians over the last forty years is rediscovering the past. The greater understanding of the past does not of course necessarily promote (still less ensure) agreement about the present or future, but it may at least generate greater tolerance.

Second, Tradition
Tradition can produce a society which is simply incapable

of viewing itself historically. There is an interesting analysis of this phenomenon in a study by Louis Rubin of a novel – *The Last Gentleman* – by Walker Percy.[8] The father in the novel – from the American South – kills himself because he cannot reconcile his ideal of aristocratic virtue with the compromises of contemporary life. The past has become for him a static, changeless icon, a pervasive heritage of order and form and community with which he identifies totally. Lives so moulded, says Rubin, become a rearguard action against any accommodation with change. Each generation needs to make its own reassessment, to translate old assumptions into usable idiom. It has to recognise that both the old idiom and the need for the new are part of a complex fabric of social experience which itself is woven by time.

Third, Myth

I doubt if any society can live without Myth. By myth I obviously do not mean either illusion or lie. I mean a large, controlling image that gives some philosophical meaning to the facts of ordinary life and provides a means for organizing experience.[9] It inevitably relies heavily on the idiom of Tradition. It is heavily charged with values and aspirations. It can engender loyalty within a group and enable it to defend itself. It can also engender hostility to those who do not share the myth, by narrowing as well as shaping our vision of reality.

Reinforced by rhetoric, it can prove a powerful tool of national cohesion and personal, social and cultural identity. Witness the French rhetoric of national unity post 1789, often masking deep divisions within the society. Most outstanding example of all is the rhetoric of American identity, reflecting the early settlers' vision of a chosen people, taking possession of their promised land and fulfilling the American dream in the successive waves of frontier development. Take just one wonderful example from Thoreau: 'There is more day to dawn. The sun is but a morning star'. A significant achievement of the American experience was to define the national identity so strongly as to enable it to accommodate the cultural pluralism which is also a feature of the society. President Bush's Inaugural reflected the point: 'In crucial things unity; in important things diversity'.

The past's role in the formation of myth is to provide a collage of images, a series of memory bytes. Brian Friel, in his play, *Translations*, put it this way: 'It is not the literal past, the "facts" of history, that shape us, but images of the past embodied in language . . . . we must never cease renewing those images, because once we do, we fossilise'.

The need for renewal of images is relevant for Ireland and not least for Northern Ireland. It is a painful process for the participants, who are inevitably caught in a veritable intellectual riptide. Initially these may be *separate* acts of renewal by the two communities. But we should not ignore the role of *myth* in promoting *cohesion*, bearing in mind that myth is often an attempt to reconcile intolerable contradictions. If such an effort at myth-making were successful, one would be close to what the poet David Gascoyne in a memorable line called 'zero hour . . . . Tomb of what was, womb of what is to be'.

In such an approach there could be a basis for the regionalism which the Ulster poet, John Hewitt, wrote about over 40 years ago. He argued that 'out of . . . loyalty to our own place, rooted in honest history, in familiar folkways and knowledge, phrased in our own dialect, there should emerge a culture and an attitude individual and distinctive, a fine contribution to the European inheritance . . . . ' [10]

May I presume to suggest that Americans have a potentially very significant part to play in promoting the kind of cohesion which my previous remarks envisage. I am aware, of course, of the generous efforts being made by Americans through the Ireland Funds, the International Fund for Ireland, the Irish American Partnership and other agencies to assist the process of peace and reconciliation and to stimulate cultural, social and economic development. I have a rather different point to make. If it rests on mistaken assumptions, I shall gladly accept correction.

I have long been a keen student of American history and affairs, but in recent months I have been taking a particular interest in the Irish diaspora and its contribution to the development of the United States. As I read the American literature, I am struck by the fact that only one significant book[11] covers the (mainly Ulster Protestant) 18th century emigration as well as the major (largely Catholic) exodus of the 1840s and beyond. For convenience I shall follow traditional usage and call the early emigrants the 'Scotch-Irish' and the later emigrants the 'Irish-Americans'.[12] Most recent American studies of which I am aware deal almost exclusively with the 19th century and the Irish-Americans.

The reason for this seems to be twofold. First, the ethnic group which had their origins in Ulster in the 18th century were by the end of that century integral parts of the American nation. Thereafter, if any man left his impress on American life, he did it as the individual he was, not as a member of the Scotch-Irish community.[13] Second, apart from the higher profile adopted by the Scotch-Irish element in the latter part of the 19th century, they seem, with limited exceptions, to have lost the kind of distinctive identity maintained by the Irish-American community. The period of higher profile to which I refer resulted (to use Carl Wittke's words) in some 'ardently filiopietistic and uncritically laudatory' literature. Nonetheless, says Wittke, 'the conclusion is inescapable that (the Scotch-Irish) made a notable and lasting contribution to the history of this nation'.[14]

This group, like the Irish American group, now constitutes some 5% of the American population.[15] Many of them are descendants of the 200,000 or more Ulster Presbyterians who left between 1700 and 1776 and of the large Scotch-Irish component of the 1.3 million Irish Protestants who emigrated thereafter. By 1790 perhaps 50% or more of the settlers on the trans-Appalachian frontier were of Ulster lineage and by the end of the century one-sixth of the total European population of the United States claimed Scotch-Irish descent. Prior to the Ulster emigration, the population of the colonies had been fairly static. The Scotch-Irish immigrants set in motion forces of national expansion. Their pattern of settlement and their economic role strengthened the connective tissue between the States. Their role in the westward advance of the frontier is undisputed. Less well-known is their contribution to the ante-bellum economy in the Southern States. There, according to recent scholarly research, they formed the backbone of a livestock sector that in 1860 was worth twice the value of the South's cotton crop.

The earlier, adulatory accounts of the Scotch-Irish tended to keep score of the exploits and achievements of individuals as bearers of distinctive racial characteristics. The archetypal figure was a composite of President Andrew Jackson, Davy Crockett and General Stonewall Jackson, of whom it was said that his favourite occupations were prayin' and fightin' (but the latter never on a Sunday). They were people who could cause an exasperated New Englander to castigate them as 'the most God-provoking Democrats this side of Hell'.

More typical of the modern approach is the contention of a greatly respected academic that 'their major lasting contribution to the American scene was their broad imprint on the American landscape and way of life . . . . in their shaping of the patterns of settlement, land-use, economy and society'. The Scotch-Irish who pioneered the Old West 'were militant moralists, and free enterprise was raised to the level of a theological dogma'.[16]

Arthur Link, the great biographer of Woodrow Wilson, wrote: 'This tiny island of Ireland has made, during the past three centuries, a greater contribution to the character and development of the American people than any other territory of comparable size and population on the face of the earth'.[17] He was talking about the *total* Irish diaspora. And that is my point. This great achievement was the work of *both* traditions, one in which they can take *joint* pride. But each tradition looks to *its own part* of the exodus and the links between the Irish-American ethnic group and Ireland are much more visible and, I feel, much stronger than is the case with the Scotch-Irish group. Of course I state a broad thesis and there are no doubt many exceptions.

The successful achievement of an explicitly and overtly *integrated* community of interest within the United States, seeking to promote peace, reconciliation and prosperity in Ireland, would constitute a powerful symbol and convey a powerful message. It would revive the situation in the early 19th century in the United States when, as one historian has put it, the striking feature about group-consciousness was that immigrants from every part of Ireland shared a sense of fellow-feeling. This of course reflected some of the political sentiment at home during that period. The demonstration effect of such a remarkable achievement for relations between the communities in Ireland could scarcely be other than beneficial. The impact on the Protestant psyche of what would in effect be the recovery of a virtually lost tribe could well be significant.

It may be appropriate to say a few words here about Northern Ireland's economic situation. Our image, amongst the uninformed, is of a traditional industrial area in decline, with the characteristics of run-down environment and poor human resource capability which normally accompany that condition – and with all the negative factors compounded by pervasive violence and political instability. This is to distort reality. In fact, most of the old industrial structure (which was highly successful and entrepreneurial in its day) has gone. There is now a strong core of modern companies trading successfully in these islands and much further afield. The old entrepreneurial flair has not been lost. One in six manufacturing jobs, employing 17,000 people, is in the more than 2,000 surviving new firms established as a result of indigenous enterprise between 1973 and 1986. Big international companies like Du Pont and Ford continue to prosper. The social and physical infrastructure relevant to industry's needs is of high quality. The arts have flourished over the last 20 years in a quite astonishing way. To provide proper perspective, all this has to be set alongside the turbulent image of recent years.

Our trouble is that there is simply not nearly enough economic activity to match a young, growing population and to mop up the unemployment which is partly a legacy of the transition to a modern economy and of the economic blizzard of the mid 70s and early 80s. Unemployment inevitably breeds social deprivation and we have far too much of both.

A burgeoning of enterprise from within – by individuals and communities – is vitally necessary. But inward investment is also critically important – and the recent decisions by the Korean company Daewoo and the French company Montupet to invest in Northern Ireland were highly significant. Only by deploying every possibility can we make real inroads into the job needs of disadvantaged areas like West Belfast. A region with an overall unemployment level of 15-20%, reaching 2 or 3 times that level in concentrated pockets of disadvantage, cannot give enough of its citizens the stake in society which makes peace and reconciliation a durable prospect.

American investment has been an encouragingly stable component of the industrial scene in Northern Ireland. Strongly reinforced, it could provide precisely the kind of industrial muscle which is needed by the less wealthy regions of Europe (like Northern Ireland) if the gap between rich and poor is not to widen still further after 1992. I am sure that that statement is equally applicable to the rest of Ireland.

It is fortunate that suggesting that American companies might like to check out such investment opportunities goes with the grain of those companies' own current stance on Europe. In a Bank of Boston poll of 1200 chief executives of manufacturing companies, over half intended to change their marketing and production strategies to exploit what they perceived as a chance to expand their sales and operations in Europe post 1992. Another survey of 200 chief executives of companies with average annual sales of 1.8 billion dollars revealed that 42% had launched a search for acquisitions or mergers and 41% a search for joint ventures.[18]

That leads me to a few concluding comments which I wish to make on Europe.

There are times when a cigar is just a cigar. That remark has been attributed to Sigmund Freud, who did more than most to deprive such objects of their simple meaning. The cigar probably most charged with meaning in Irish literature was the one which Robert Hall got from Richard Rowan in James Joyce's play *Exiles*. Robert says: 'These cigars Europeanise me. If Ireland is to become a New Ireland, she must first become European'.[19]

This bears a strong resemblance to a remark by Thomas Kettle, except that Kettle writes about the need to become European in order to 'become deeply Irish'. He believed that the distinctive character of nations is fashioned not in isolation but in the mainstream of civilisation. 'All cultures', he said, 'belong to a nation that has once taken sure hold of its own culture'. Elaborating this, he said: 'while a strong people has its own self for centre, it has the universe for circumference'. This reads the banns for an easy *cultural* marriage between national heritage and the European ideal. We must, of course, add in regional identity to make an agreeable ménage à trois.

The *political* relationships may be more difficult to arrange. Whatever the outcome, I believe that the residual authority relevant to the regions is likely to continue to reside with the nation state rather than migrate to a larger and more remote European entity, since a valid regional policy entails the shaping of the *entirety* of public policy in terms of regional needs. Current regional policy issuing from European Community institutions diverges little from conventional regional policy in nation states hitherto. *So long as this is so*, it is difficult – generally speaking – to see what European institutions can do for the regions which their national Governments cannot do *if* there are adequate arrangements for resource transfers between states within Europe and *if* the development of disadvantaged regions is made a Community priority. Such priority would call for a *proactive industrial* policy to ensure that, in the development of the Single Market, the regional imperative is *factored into* the operation of market forces rather than regarded as an *exception to* the operation of market forces.

I appreciate that the programmes being devised under the Structural Funds are intended to address the development needs of regions comprehensively. But this falls short of acceptance by the European Community of a responsibility to *skew* a disproportionate share of growth in Europe towards disadvantaged regions. The traditional weapons of regional policy, operating largely on the supply side of the economic equation, are vitally important and regions must project and market themselves vigorously and avoid the mentality of dependency. But none of this on its own may be enough to counter the 'drag' effect of geographical peripherality (which is a fact) and of distance (which is largely perception).

Whatever happens in Europe, the regions need more autonomy to develop their own personalities. They need more effective means of contributing to national policy debates and expressing their preferences and priorities. The spring which holds in tension the tendencies towards the single and the plural in our constitutional arrangements needs to be relaxed in favour of the diversity of local community.

This is why the prospect of devolved Government in Northern Ireland is so exciting and why it is so important that the political debate there should focus as much on the purposes of power as on the path to power and the apparatus of power. This is also why myth as 'creative symbol' (in Richard Kearney's phrase) is so relevant. It may be true, as Kettle said, that we Irish have a tendency to exhaust, in *depicting* utopias, the energies which might better be spent in *creating* them. Even so, people of different traditions in Northern Ireland might do worse than concert their energies to depict a few utopias.

Footnotes

1. Richard Kearney, *Myth and Motherland*, in *Ireland's Field Day* (Hutchinson, 1985).
2. Joseph Lee, Whither Ireland: The Next Twenty-Five Years, in *Ireland in Transition*, ed. K. A. Kennedy (Mercier Press, 1986).
3. References here and elsewhere are to Thomas Kettle, *The Day's Burden and Other Essays*, (Gill and Macmillan, 1968).
4. In this and the preceding paragraph I draw on Aaron Wildavsky, *The Art and Craft of Policy Analysis*, (Macmillan, 1980).
5. See T. Peters and R. H. Waterman, *In Search of Excellence*; Tom Peters, *Thriving on Chaos*; Robert H. Waterman, *The Renewal Factor*.
6. Plato, *The Republic*, trans. by H. D. P. Lee (Penguin Books, 1955).
7. See Declan Kiberd, *Anglo-Irish Attitudes*, in *Ireland's Field Day* (Hutchinson, 1985).
8. Essay by Louis D. Rubin in *The American South: Portrait of a Culture*, Edited by Louis D. Rubin (Louisiana State University Press, 1980).
9. This follows closely the definition by Mark Schorer, quoted in George B. Tindall, *Mythology: A New Frontier in Southern History* in *Myth and Southern History* edited by Patrick Gerster and Nicholas Cords (Rand McNally College Publishing Company, 1974), on which I draw for this paragraph.
10. John Hewitt, *Regionalism: The Last Chance*, in *Ancestral Voices*, edited by Tom Clyde (The Blackstaff Press, 1987).
11. Kerby A. Millar, *Emigrants and Exiles* (Oxford, 1985).
12. I am of course aware that the early emigration also encompassed Catholics as well as Protestants who were not Scotch-Irish and that the later emigration included substantial numbers of non-Catholics.
13. This line of argument is pursued in James G. Leyburn, *The Scotch-Irish: A Social History* (Chapel Hill, 1962), who largely for this reason concerns himself mainly with the period up to the American War of Independence.
14. Carl Wittke, *The Irish in America* (edition reissued by Russell and Russell, 1970).
15. Andrew M. Greeley, *The Irish Americans* (Harper and Row, 1981).
16. E. Estyn Evans, *The Scotch-Irish: Their Cultural Adaptation and Heritage in the American Old West*, in E. R. R. Green (ed.) *Essays in Scotch-Irish History* (Routledge and Kegan Paul, 1969).
17. Arthur S. Link, *Woodrow Wilson and His Presbyterian Inheritance*, in E. R. R. Green (ed.) *Essays in Scotch-Irish History* (Routledge and Kegan Paul, 1969).
18. Surveys reported in *The Economist*, May 13, 1989.
19. Cf. Sean O'Faolain, *The Great O'Neill* (Longman, 1942). O'Faolain saw O'Neill as a European figure, living 'through Ireland into Europe, out of this remote island into the ubiquitous and contemporaneous world of civilised mind' and providing 'all future nationalism with [the] purple and gold' of a rich European heritage – or at least the opportunity of access to it. O'Faolain was clearly sceptical about the extent to which the opportunity had been grasped.

The Origins of Mass Emigration from Ireland

GRAEME KIRKHAM

Human migration – the uprooting of individuals, families, sometimes whole societies, to journey to a new home – is a process particularly susceptible to myth-making. Nowhere more so than in Ireland, where the history of population movement across the Atlantic, to Britain, Europe and Australasia, over a period of three centuries or more, has been subject to a greater extent than most areas of the past to the play of emotion and partisan feeling. The word 'emigration' has immediate connotations of 'coffin-ships', poverty, hunger and historical oppressions. The rise of a new professional scholarship in Irish history over the past three decades has changed academic understanding, but popular perceptions of Irish emigration history remain fixed on the exodus of the mid-nineteenth century. These images colour perceptions of the past and distort popular reactions to contemporary emigration.

Yet Irish emigration has a considerably longer pedigree; the vast outflow of population during the Famine period marked a change in scale, not the advent of something new in Irish society. This paper is intended to provide a brief view of Irish migration in the period before 1700, and then to assess the origins of mass emigration as a distinct and important Irish social phenomenon during the first half of the eighteenth century.

I

The emergence of an Atlantic economy in the seventeenth century, based on the exploitation of new lands and new commodities, created novel demands for labour, settlers,

81

entrepreneurs and military and maritime personnel. Numerically, Ireland contributed most heavily to the first of these categories: from at least the 1620s Irish indentured servants and transported vagrants and felons formed a substantial part of the labour force in the Caribbean islands and the tobacco plantations of Virginia and Maryland. In the late 1660s, for example, there were at least 12,000 Irish in the West Indies, of whom 8,000 were in Barbados. These were surviving populations: mortality rates were high and the total numbers who had made the transatlantic voyage were substantially larger. What proportions of these migrants departed willingly or were coerced is unknown. Certainly not all were labourers: at about the same time some ten per cent of property holders in Jamaica were of Irish origin.

With the rise of slave importation, the movement of Irish to the Caribbean declined, but the traffic into the tobacco colonies continued into the eighteenth century. Other Irish migrants, in relatively small numbers, appeared in most of the mainland American colonies during the seventeenth century. Even in strongly anti-Catholic New England there was an identifiable population of Irish servants in the second half of this period. In contrast to the later period, however, the proportion of Irish migrants who sailed as free, unbound, fare-paying passengers, with the intention of settling as farmers or tradesmen, was minor.

This transatlantic movement of the seventeenth century foreshadowed the much greater movement of later periods and is important as an example of the way in which Ireland had already been drawn into the developing world economy centred on European expansion. However, the numbers of Irish who crossed to Europe were almost certainly considerably larger than those going to America or the Caribbean. The major economic and social dislocations which resulted from religious and political change in seventeenth-century Ireland, together with the opportunities provided by the many Continental wars of the period, prompted many thousands of Irishmen to enter military service as officers, regular soldiers or mercenaries in the armies of France, Spain, Austria, the Spanish Netherlands, Poland, Denmark and Sweden. Dispossessed members of the former Catholic Irish elite found themselves able to retain a degree of status, not open to them in Ireland, in several European courts. For those who wished to follow them, or were merely adventurous and found opportunity lacking in Ireland, Europe became a haven.

Also of importance was the Irish religious establishment in Europe. Theological colleges provided opportunities for the training of priests and other Catholic clergy, and during periods of official repression of the Catholic church in Ireland many clerics escaped or were deported to the Continent. In 1653 alone more than a thousand were said to have departed from Ireland. Many newly ordained priests and expelled clergy returned, but there were many who did not, forming distinct Irish communities in seminaries and colleges throughout Europe.

Another notable group were the Irish merchants who settled and traded in most of the major ports of the Atlantic coasts of France and Spain. Dealing in imports of Irish butter, beef and hides, and exports of wines and brandy, many diversifying into colonial trade with the West Indies, this mercantile population persisted over a long period. In the latter part of the eighteenth century there were 60 Irish merchant houses in Bordeaux, for example, and more than 40 in Cadiz; the presence of the Irish name Hennessy on a major Franch brandy is a legacy of these Irish trading colonies.

The other major destination for Irish migrants of the seventeenth century was Britain, although less is known of this movement than of others to more distant parts. Geographic proximity and relative ease of travel particularly encouraged outflows to England and Scotland at periods of food shortage or economic recession, as, for example, in the first few years of the seventeenth century and in the late 1620s. By the early eighteenth century there were substantial settled Irish communities in many of the larger British cities, and continuing Irish immigration. In 1736 there were major riots in London, with mobs attacking Irish-owned inns and houses, because of the employment of Irish building workers on a new church and the large numbers of Irish weavers working for low wages in the silk industry; one master weaver alone was said to employ almost 200. In the same year, Irish agricultural labourers seeking to escape from depresed economic conditions at home were routed from some country areas in the south of England by the local populations, again fearful of losing their own employment to the migrant strangers.

It is not possible to make any solid quantitative assessment of the scale of movement out of Ireland during the seventeenth century. Yet it is clear that it was not negligible and that it affected a range of social groups within Irish society. It also affected many regions of the country, although servants for the West Indies and the mainland American colonies were probably drawn predominantly from the areas around the ports of the south and south west most heavily involved in transatlantic trade. Migrants to Britain probably came from these same port hinterlands, but also from Leinster and Ulster. In contrast with the succeeding period, however, the movement tended to be sporadic, piecemeal and unstructured. Those departing were predominantly male: the relatively small number of women involved goes a long way towards explaining the failure of the migrations of this period to create distinctive and persistent Irish settlements in all but a few of the destination areas.

II

Eighteenth-century emigration from Ireland drew most heavily on the province of Ulster, and the myth-making process referred to at the beginning of this paper has afflicted the history of the flow from the north of Ireland to America to an extent perhaps greater than for any other population movement of the past. The chroniclers of the 'Scotch-Irish' have generated an enormous literature, much of it of greater polemic content than historical value. Something of the flavour of this campaign to assert the pre-eminence of Ulster emigrants in the rise of America and to establish a separate 'Scotch-Irish' ethnic identity can be understood from the title of a minor work published in 1899, James Shaw's *The Scotch Irish in History as the Master Builders of Empires, States, Churches, Schools and Civilisation*.

Only in the past 25 years has a more balanced and objective view of the period emerged through the work of R. J. Dickson, Audrey Lockhart, David Doyle, Kerby Miller and other specialist historians. In seeking causes for the eighteenth-century outflow from Ulster the former emphasis on religious and political oppressions has diminished and greater attention given to underlying economic factors. Whereas it was formerly proposed that Ulster Presbyterians composed almost the entirety of eighteenth-century migrants from Ireland, it is now seen that the exodus from the north was only part of a greater outflow. An estimated 350,000 people left Ireland in the three-quarters of a century before the American Revolution; emigrants from Ulster undoubtedly constituted the largest proportion of these, and northern Protestants certainly departed in numbers wholly disproportionate to their share of Irish population, but there were significant migrations from other regions as well. Nonetheless, the striking feature of the movement from Ulster was that in the period before about 1750 it developed a specific character and continuity in a way which previous outflows, and contemporary movements from other areas, did not. During this period, one part of Ireland saw the regular emigration of individuals to North America on a substantial scale become for the first time an established element in its economic and social life.

The years around 1718 have been seen as marking a beginning to Ulster emigration, but it seems probable that the real origins of the link between the province and colonial America lie a generation or more earlier. In the last two decades of the seventeenth century there was a small scale movement of settlers to Maryland and to the newly opened settlements of the Carolinas, New Jersey and the Quaker colony of Pennsylvania; there may also have been a movement to New England. This was a period of considerable economic and political disruption in Ireland, but migration was also promoted by the efforts made by the proprietors of the colonies to plant settlers on their lands. Overall numbers of emigrants during this period are difficult to determine, and are unlikely to have exceeded a few thousand. More importantly, however, it was during these years that popular awareness first emerged in Ulster of America as a possible refuge from present tribulations at home.

The economy of Ireland as a whole was depressed during the first half of the eighteenth century, but Ulster was particularly vulnerable. The province underwent a period of economic and social strain as it moved rapidly from an underdeveloped agricultural base to an economy solidly founded on domestic industry, in which a large proportion of the population were dependent on the well-being of the linen industry and purchased at least part of their basic food supplies from the market. During this period major surges of migration occurred in the years 1717-19, 1727-29, 1735-36, 1740-41 and 1745-46, all prompted by economic distress and poor harvests. About half of all the identified voyages of emigrant vessels from Ulster in the 40 years before 1750 took place in such 'problem' years. Other regions in Ireland experienced similar surges during some of these periods, although on a considerably smaller scale.

The importance of economic downturns and harvest crises in prompting emigration should not be interpreted to mean that at such times embarkation for America was necessarily an escape from imminent starvation; rather that in a non-accumulation oriented society such as this, any sudden rise in food prices or lowering of the returns from agricultural output or domestic industry immediately unbalanced household budgets intended to provide a comfortable equilibrium between income and expenditure in normal seasons. At such times the burden of rents and tithes in Ulster seemed particularly onerous, the cheap land of America particularly attractive. In these circumstances the transatlantic passage became an extension of the normal crisis migration pattern of a pre-industrial economy: people could now run from hard times all the way to America.

Of course, not all emigrants were prompted by economic difficulties or the threat of imminent hardship; for many others, ambition, adventure or simple curiosity provided adequate reason. The letters sent home by previous migrants, combined with other sources of information such as newspaper advertisements, handbills and the perorations in favour of emigration made by ships' masters and their agents at fairs and markets, ensured that popular knowledge of America was widespread.

This factor provides an additional element in the solution of the puzzle of the imbalance between Protestant and Catholic emigration from Ireland to America which existed from the early eighteenth century until the 1830s. Kerby Miller has argued for major differences in cultural perceptions of emigration between the two groups. The specific invitations extended to Protestant settlers and, conversely, the lack of welcome for Catholic migrants in many of the colonies were also important, although numbers of Catholics nevertheless went. Additionally, however, it is clear that given the much higher literacy rates among Protestants of the period, letters and printed materials were considerably more likely to influence this group. Language may also have played a part; many Ulster Catholics, particularly in more remote areas, were monoglot Irish speakers. This would not only have impeded the flow of information to them but also made them less eligible as potential emigrants to a predominantly English-speaking society.

Demand for emigration must have been determined to some extent by the cost of the passage. Unfortunately, solid information on fares charged to emigrants during the first half of the eighteenth century is almost entirely absent. R. J. Dickson has suggested that competition and the integration of emigration with other elements of maritime trade resulted in a reduction of fares in the period between the 1720s and 1770s, but it should be added that increasing household incomes from involvement in domestic industry may in any case have made it easier for individuals and families to find the necessary cash sums. An alternative option for some was the sale of the 'interest', or right of renewal, on the lease of a farm holding; in large areas of Ulster rising land values enabled tenants selling their lease interests to realise substantial sums.

However, the emigration option was not restricted to those who could afford the fare, for a large, although not readily quantifiable proportion of those who made the voyage did so as indentured servants. These individuals bargained their lives and labour for a period of four or five years in return for a passage to America. Once arrived, their services were sold to farmers, urban tradesmen and others in a market where labour was in considerable demand. For many of these individuals, clearly, the passage opened new horizons of opportunity in trade, commerce or land ownership which were not available at home. Other migrants travelled as redemptioners, promising to repay the cost of passage within a specified period after arrival; many of these hoped to obtain the necessary sums from relatives already settled in America; others sold themselves or their children as servants on arrival to find the cost.

If these elements combined to create a body of prospective emigrants, then other factors provided the necessary supply of passages. During the first half of the eighteenth century the whole process of population movement from Ulster to America became progressively commercialized, a constituent part in the Atlantic maritime economy. Many of the earliest identifiable voyages of emigrant ships can be identified as special charter operations, or as speculative ventures by merchants hoping to find a profitable return cargo to an American port. Increasingly, however, the westward voyage of vessels carrying migrants from Ulster ports to Philadelphia, New York, Charleston or Boston fitted into a complex pattern of trade. At the simplest level, ships carried flax seed, flour or timber from America to Ireland, and then returned with a complement of passengers, repeating these voyages season after season. Other vessels called at Ulster ports for emigrants while en route from British ports or from Dublin, supplementing their lading of manufactured goods. The most singular pattern of trade to include Ulster emigrant passages was followed by a number of New York vessels: these brought flax seed to an Ulster port and there embarked servants and passengers; however, instead of returning directly across the Atlantic the ships then proceeded to the Isle of May, off the north-west coast of Africa, for a cargo of salt before sailing for America.

By the 1740s some of the vessels transporting emigrants had apparently been designed and built to cater for the demands of passenger-carrying, and promised – in their advertisements if not on board – some degree of comfort. The *William and James*, advertised to sail from Belfast to the Delaware in 1739, was described as 'well-fitted, and of excellent Accommodations; being a new ship, built for the trade, and very commodious for carrying Passengers'; the *Frances and Elizabeth* claimed 'extraordinary accommodations for passengers' when she sailed from Philadelphia for Derry in 1742, and the *Jenny*, set for Philadelphia from Derry in 1750, was presented as 'very commodious for passengers (being fully five foot high between decks)'. The *Hibernia*, advertising passages from Philadelphia to Belfast in 1752, was described as 'intended for the Irish trade, and . . . well accommodated for passengers; they may depend on the best usage'.

Many of the emigrant vessels were certainly relatively new. Of a sample of 20 ships recorded in the period 1732-45 for which such data are available, 14 were five years old or less, of which five were in their first or second seasons afloat. The size of vessels involved in the trade also increased. The average registered tonnage of emigrant vessels rose from 55 tons in the 1710s to almost 70 tons in the 1740s. Nevertheless, some of the vessels plying the Atlantic during the first half of the century were considerably smaller than these averages. The *Speedwell*, a sloop of only 18 tons, arrived in New York from Belfast in 1732, captained by William Cross; five years later the same master arrived in Philadelphia after a voyage from Derry in the 15 ton schooner *Revenge*.

Transatlantic crossings clearly bore an element of risk, but this may have been exacerbated in the early period by lack of experience in masters and crews. In 1729, towards the end of a major wave of crisis migration from Ulster, the *Pennsylvania Gazette* had warned of 'long and miserable passages, occasioned probably by the unskilfulness of the mariners; the people, earnest to be gone, being obliged to take any vessel that will go; and 'tis frequently with such as have before been only coasters, because they cannot always get those that have been used to long voyages to these parts of the world . . . . ' In the succeeding period, shipping records show numbers of masters and vessels making regular annual transatlantic crossings from Ulster to America, and both ships and their captains began to gain marketable reputations. Captain William Blair, master of the *William and Mary* of Philadelphia, was described in 1746 as 'well known and remarkable for his Success these many years in this Voyage'. The *Jenny*, cited above, was promoted in 1750 as having made 'two voyages to Philadelphia this last Season, and has been very successful'. In the same year, James Irvine, master of the Coleraine-owned vessel *Nancy*, promised somewhat ambiguously to 'give as good Treatment as he has done heretofore'.

Even with an experienced master, however, the passage to America still held many dangers. The *Happy Return*, for example, made annual voyages between Derry and Philadelphia in the years 1742 to 1747; in the latter year the vessel ran onto a shoal on the American coast at the end of the crossing and 50 of her passengers were drowned. In January 1747 the ship *Catherine* arrived in Philadelphia on her fifth westward crossing in two and a half years. On this voyage the vessel had been taken by a French privateer and ransomed for £500; on the return trip to Derry, laden with a valuable cargo, she was boarded again off the Donegal coast and ransomed for £1300. The ship *Arundel* arrived at Newcastle-on-Delaware in 1746 after a passage of three and a half months, during which the captain, both mates and a number of passengers had died; during the crossing she had been taken by a Spanish privateer who carried off two of the Ulster emigrants on board as hostages for a ransom of 4000 pieces of eight.

These were dangers inherent in all long distance sea travel during the period. Despite them, the volume of emigration increased steadily. It seems probable that by 1750 at least 50,000 Ulster migrants had already made the voyage to America. This is a small total by comparison with the numbers who left in the second half of the century, and during most of the nineteenth century the figure was exceeded many times over by annual totals of migrants, year after year. Equally, the emigration trade grew in complexity of organization and in commercial significance after 1750. However, the real importance of the statistic may be judged from the fact that at the mid-eighteenth century the population of Ulster was between 500,000 and 600,000; if 50,000 people emigrated from the province in a period of less than two generations, then a large part of the population, particularly the Protestant portion, must have had some close personal tie with an individual or family who had made the voyage across the Atlantic and perhaps made good. When those left behind subsequently experienced the burdens of poor harvests or economic depression, or were fired by the pricks of ambition or an adventurous spirit, an alternative to life in Ulster was not difficult to identify or to achieve.

*Part of the research on which this paper is based was carried out by the author for the Garfield Weston Research Project, 'Emigration from Ulster to North America', at the University of Ulster at Coleraine, 1982-85.

Information on Irish emigration during the period discussed is to be found in a number of articles by the author and in the following: J. J. Silke, 'The Irish abroad, 1534-1691', in T. W. Moody, F. X. Martin and F. J. Byrne (eds.), *A New History of Ireland, Vol. III: Early Modern Ireland, 1534-1691* (Oxford, 1978), 587-633; R. J. Dickson, *Ulster Emigration to Colonial America, 1718-1775* (Belfast, 1988; reprint of 1976 edition with new introduction by G. Kirkham); Audrey Lockhart, *Some Aspects of Emigration from Ireland to the North American Colonies between 1660 and 1775* (New York, 1976); D. N. Doyle, *Ireland, Irishmen and Revolutionary America, 1760-1820* (Dublin, 1981); K. A. Miller, *Emigrants and Exiles: Ireland and the Irish Exodus to North America* (Oxford, 1985).

Emigration, Capitalism, and Ideology in Post-Famine Ireland[1]

In the late 19th and 20th centuries, economic and social changes
in Ireland consigned approximately three out of every four
Irishmen and women born in that period to the emigrant ships
and, often, to the slums of American and British cities. Their
reasons for emigrating were essentially similar or identical to
those which produced mass migration from other European
countries: for example, the decline of cottage industries, crop
failures, falling agricultural prices, the exigencies of impartible
inheritance and the dowry system, and the increasing redun-
dancy of petty farmers and agricultural labourers brought about
by the consolidation of holdings, the conversion of tillage to
pasture, and the introduction of labour- and cost-saving farm
machinery – in short, to the development of Irish capitalism
which, along with its cultural consequences, has been given the
more neutral or benign labels of 'commercialization' or 'modernization'. Moreover, although Protestant landlords,
businessmen, and professionals dominated the Irish economy
during the 19th century, many of the most compelling causes of
emigration were generated within the Catholic community,
especially by its emerging middle class of affluent farmers and
townsmen. This was especially true during the post-famine
period (1856-1929) when most departures occurred, and it is
problematic how much suffering and emigration among the rural
lower classes (labourers, smallholders, farmers' noninheriting
children) were really more attributable to profit-maximization
among Catholic graziers, strong farmers, and rural parents,
generally, than to Protestant landlords or British officials.
Nevertheless, although the great majority of Irish Catholic

91

emigrants left home for mundane economic reasons rooted in the dynamics and inequities of their own society, the interpretation of emigration which enjoyed greatest currency and legitimacy among Irish Catholics during the period was that of emigration as exile, as *in*voluntary expatriation, which was obliged by forces beyond both individual choice and communal control: sometimes by fate or destiny, but usually by the political and economic consequences of 'British misgovernment', 'Protestant ascendancy', and 'landlord tyranny'. However, although British policies and the landlord system set the broad parameters for the development of Irish capitalism, properly speaking the exile label was applicable only to a relatively small number of Catholic emigrants – for example, to political rebels and evicted tenants who left Ireland under peculiar duress. Furthermore, after the land acts of the 1880s Irish landlordism was fatally weakened, after 1903 rapidly abolished, and in the same period the British parliament granted the Irish substantial self-government and funds for economic development. However, the explanation of emigration as political exile remained prevalent, still colouring the letters and memoirs of ordinary Catholic emigrants as well as songs and ballads, political speeches, and clerical sermons. This was because for several reasons, both archaic and contemporary, the misperception of emigration as political banishment was integral to Catholic Irishmen's sense of individual and collective identity and, most important, it was crucial for maintaining 'social stability' and bourgeoise hegemony in a Catholic society whose capitalist institutions and social relationships made mass lower-class emigration imperative.

Sources of the Exile Motif
First, the notion of emigration as exile was rooted deeply in Irish literary and historical tradition. Long before the Norman invasion, Gaelic poets commonly employed the word *deoraí* (literally, *exile*) to describe anyone who left Ireland for any reason. Given the impact of later, more thorough English conquests, it was natural that 17th- and 18th-century bards applied *deoraí* and similar terms to the fates of O'Neill, Sarsfield, and their expatriate followers – thereby providing seemingly apposite models for subsequent, ordinary emigrants.

Second, the idea that emigration was communal necessity rather than, say, individual opportunity for self-betterment perfectly reflected a prevalent tendency in the traditional Irish Catholic worldview to devalue individual action, ambition, and the assumption of personal responsibility – especially when actions, such as emigration, seemed innovative and threatening to customary patterns of behaviour and thought which enjoined, by example and precept, passive or communal values such as duty, continuity, and conformity. This worldview was rooted in the secular, religious, and linguistic aspects of traditional Gaelic culture, and, although confirmed by conquests and confiscations, both antedated and transcended those experiences. In terms of the secular aspects of pre- and post-conquest Catholic society, ideally and, to a great extent, practically, that society was hierarchical, communal, familial, and traditional – and each emphasis diminished the individual's responsibility and importance in relation to society. Likewise, the religious aspects of Irish culture reinforced the temporal constraints and sacralized their emphases on obedience to collective authority; this was true of both pre-modern or 'peasant' religion, with its fairy-belief and 'predictive celebrations', and the more formal and hermetically-sealed system imposed through the 19th-century 'devotional revolution'. Also, the Irish language in its semantic structure makes sharp distinctions between active and passive states of being, and, in comparison to English, classifies a much broader range of phenomena into an area in which action and self-assertion are inappropriate. Thus, the most common way for an Irish-speaker to describe emigration has been *dob éigin dom imeach go Meirice*: 'I *had* to go to America', or, more precisely, 'going to America was a necessity for me' – an impersonal interpretation entirely consistent with the use of *deoraí* (exile) to designate *emigrant*, as one subject to imposed pressures, and likewise consistent with the received images of cultural heroes such as the Ulster earls and the 'wild geese'.

Third, both the interpretation of emigration as exile and the general outlook which supported that interpretation remained common in 19th- and early 20th-century Ireland because of the contradictions and the tensions which characterized a society in rapid transition. Although contemporaries often decried the 'anglicization' of rural values which accompanied capitalist development, sometimes complaining that culturally-deracinated Irish youths no longer viewed emigration sorrowfully, the expatriate imagery and its corroboratory worldview still seemed applicable to many social realities and processes which remained eminently 'explainable' in pre-modern terms. As a result of the uneven distribution and impact of modernization, many traditional institutions, task orientations, even linguistic patterns (in Hiberno-English, as well as Gaeltacht Irish) lasted well into the 20th century. Moreover, not only did the influence of 'outsiders' (British officials, landlords) long remain potent, but within Catholic Ireland itself the disappearance of secret agrarian societies, increased clerical authority, the marginalization of farm labourers and farmers' noninheriting children, and the enmeshing of smallholders in webs of debt may have reduced, rather than widened, the scope of responsible choice enjoyed by most rural dwellers. Thus, some aspects of Irish development may not have promoted more individualistic or independent outlooks, but instead enjoined continued or even increased dependence on and deference to familial obligations, patron-client ties, and communal authority figures in order to ensure survival and status.[2]

However, although mitigated, socioeconomic and cultural changes in post-famine Ireland were great and, in some respects, swift and traumatic – especially in the western counties which produced a disproportionately large share of the exodus. Yet paradoxically, those very innovations, so pregnant with social disruption and demoralization, themselves encouraged greater popular reliance on traditional outlooks and 'explanations' which could relieve the tensions consequent on rapid transition. In order to ensure social and psychological equilibrium, changes had to be interpreted in customary, comforting ways. Thus, while most post-famine Irish responded 'rationally' to an emerging capitalism's economic exigencies or opportunities (e.g., by adopting impartible inheritance or by emigrating), they usually fell back on traditional categories of thought ('it was a necessity . . . ') to justify, exculpate, or obscure causation and accountability – sometimes, as in the case of emigration, projecting responsibility for change on uncontrollable and/or 'alien' forces. Hence, they could square traditional values and customary, communal sanctions with the actual practice of a new and broader 'freedom' of action, cloaking the rising tide of individual calculation in the assumed anonymity of explanatory strategies designed to avoid conflicts both internal and with familial, social, and religious institutions which still demanded conformity to old ideals and obligations.

Finally and most important, although such compromises between tradition and innovation were psychological necessities, the precise *forms* of such ideological adjustments – such as the fiction that all emigration was basically political exile – were determined by the new social structures and power relationships within Catholic Irish society. Although the archaic *deoraí* tradition remained vibrant in the Gaeltacht, its revived, formalized expression throughout the commercialized, English-speaking Ireland of the post-famine era served as an instrument of socioeconomic, cultural, and political hegemony for the social groups which had emerged pre-eminent from the wreckage of pre-famine society and which were not only in the forefront of capitalist development but which therefore found it most expedient and essential to explain or justify their innovations and consequent dominance in traditional categories which could inhibit resentment and resistance from those who were or felt disadvantaged by the resultant discontinuities. Put simply, in the 'New Ireland' of the post-famine period there were three dominant social institutions: first, the strong-farmer *type* of rural family (the 'stem family'), characterized by impartible inheritance, the dowry system, and postponed marriage; second, the Catholic church of the 'devotional revolution'; and third, Irish nationalism, especially in its constitutional or quasi-legal forms. All three were innovative in structure and purpose, and all were associated with the *embourgeoisement* of Catholic society – adopted by or imposed on Catholic smallholders and labourers from models of 'proper' social, religious, and political behaviour enjoined by middle-class farmers, clerics, and townsmen. All three upset or challenged traditional 'peasant' practices and outlooks – sometimes to people's obvious disadvantage, as in the case of farmers' disinherited children – yet all demanded absolute conformity and proscribed deviations as familial ingratitude, religious apostasy, or even national treason.

Essentially, these very modern institutions had to regenerate the centuries-old imagery of emigration as exile because the stem family and the primary support groups for the Church and the nationalist movement (middle-class farmers and townsmen) shared major responsibility for mass, lower-class emigration. The remainder of this essay focuses on clerical and political attitudes to emigration, but with regard to the rural family, the notion of emigration forced by fate or British oppression, rather than personal calculation, was vital in mitigating potentially explosive conflicts between parents and offspring and between inheriting and noninheriting children. However, just as the intrafamilial tensions and resolutions concerning emigration were much more complex than that brief statement suggests,[3] so also did Catholic society's 'official' spokesmen have to balance bourgeois interests and peasant or proletarian sensibilities, in the process often producing highly contradictory statements.

Emigration and the Contradictions of Catholic Nationalism
A few Catholic leaders openly acknowledged that many people's 'irredeemable poverty' made at least some emigration 'absolutely necessary', and many priests viewed their parishioners' departures with resignation. However, as the central experience of post-famine life, emigration demanded interpretation in political and religious contexts. On one hand, Catholic spokesmen often eulogized the accomplishments of the 'Irish race' overseas, and clergymen were especially prone to describe the exodus as 'divine destiny' and the emigrants as 'holy missionaries' for the Catholic faith. On the other hand, negative characterizations of emigration overwhelmingly predominated, and after the famine most clerics and nationalists united in condemning it. For Ireland as a whole emigration was seen as tragic because it deprived the island of its young men and women, its 'bone and sinew', and so threatened ultimate depopulation. Likewise, critics also charged that emigration was tragic and potentially disastrous for the emigrants themselves. Clerics, especially, espoused this argument: at first they emphasized primarily the hazards of the voyage and the poverty and physical dangers which awaited poor emigrants in the new world, but later they broadened their attack and stigmatized the United States itself as a vicious, materialistic, 'godless' society which corrupted the emigrants' morals and destroyed their faith. According to priests such as Peter O'Leary, Joseph Guinan, and Patrick Sheehan,

America was an 'unnatural land' where innocent Irish youths would be 'dragged down to shame and crime', and they urged their listeners 'to save their souls in Holy Ireland than to hazard them for this world's goods among American heretics'.

However, while agreeing that emigration was lamentable, nationalists and clergymen were very inconsistent in assigning blame for its prevalence. Some charged that the emigrants themselves were culpable, either because they were too naive to resist the blandishments of ticket brokers and returned 'Yanks',or, more harshly, because they were 'coward[s]', 'sordid churl[s]', and 'lucre-loving wretch[es], as Fanny Parnell charged in 1880, or 'traitor[s] to the Irish State' and 'deserters who have left their posts', as Patrick Pearse later claimed. However, it was much more common to blame emigration on landlordism and British oppression, and to characterize the emigrants as sorrowing, vengeful 'exiles'. Thus, according to priests such as Guinan and Thomas Burke, the emigrants were victims of religious and political persecution, while the emigrants themselves purportedly were consumed with a passionate 'love for Ireland' and a desire to 'breathe once more the peat-scented air of their native valleys'. Likewise, nearly all nationalist politicians characterized the exodus as a 'reluctant emigration' which would cease only when Ireland was independent and so able to provide prosperity and employment for all. 'Ireland has resources to feed five times her population', Pearse typically asserted, and so a 'free Ireland would not, and could not, have hunger in her fertile vales and squalor in her cities'.

Such contradictory attributions of blame for emigration reflected nationalists' and clerics' tortuous efforts to reconcile traditional social ideals and their own hegemonic imperatives with new capitalist realities which violated those ideals and yet, paradoxically, both sustained and threatened their hegemony over the Catholic masses. Save in the context of wholesale emigration by the dispossessed and disinherited, bourgeois dominance of rural Ireland could not have been achieved without immeasurably greater tension and conflict within the Catholic community, and many Catholic spokesmen realized that only the massive, lower-class exodus had created the relatively commercialized and de-Gaelicized Ireland which had been a precondition for the success of disciplined nationalist movements and of the church's 'devotional revolution'. Lower-class emigration had enabled the comparatively conflict-free consolidation of many strong farmers' and graziers' holdings, and those affluent groups and their shopkeeper allies were vital support sources for institutionalized piety and patriotism. Similarly, emigration stabilized the family farm, helped preclude overt social and generational strife over land, and prevented the subdivision, pauperization, and lower-class violence against rural 'modernizers' which had characterized the pre-famine decades. In addition, Catholic leaders also understood that emigration brought specific material benefits to key elements in the 'New Ireland'. For instance, publicans and shopkeepers – often vociferous nationalists – profited from the sale of passage tickets, while much of the £1 million in annual remittances from America found its way to the retailers' coffers and the priests' collection boxes. More crucially, Irish clerics and nationalists relied heavily on Irish-Americans' loyalty and contributions to finance church-building, agitation, and, ultimately, insurrection at home. In short, Catholic spokesmen had good reasons to praise the emigrants and to rationalize the exodus as the 'Divine Mission of the Irish Race'.

However, Irish nationalists had to denounce emigration for more compelling reasons. Emigration connoted depopulation, and ever since the early 19th century, when British economists urged wholesale removal of Ireland's 'surplus' inhabitants, the issue of Irish population had been charged with politics and emotion; in that context, both the famine clearances and more recent evictions, as during the Land War, made the equation of all emigration with planned 'extermination' seem logical, if ahistorical. Moreover, emigration endangered nationalists' hopes for Ireland's future and their efforts to oppose British authority and anglicizing influences. For example, the further development of Irish capitalism seemed threatened by the drain of potential entrepreneurs, workers, and consumers. More important, many leaders feared that mass departures were undermining Catholic Ireland's religious and political bulwarks by either eroding church membership or providing a safety valve for discontent which otherwise could be mobilized against British rule. Thus, in 1920 the Dáil's minister of defence issued a manifesto warning that the British government was attempting to stimulate emigration and thereby weaken the national struggle: 'The young men of Ireland must stand fast', he demanded, for 'to leave their country at this supreme crisis would be nothing less than base desertion in the face of the enemy'. Also, Catholic leaders were apprehensive lest emigration deprive them of political and religious influence over the emigrants themselves, especially if they left home for 'selfish', materialistic reasons. Lay nationalists feared that emigrants 'were casting off all allegiance to the motherland', while churchmen were concerned about the danger of apostasy or 'spiritual ruin' overseas.

Hence, their self-assumed roles as Ireland's champions obliged Catholic spokesmen to denounce emigration: as bishop George Butler of Limerick put it in 1864, in a letter to fellow churchmen, 'The depopulation of our country is progressing at an awful pace and *we must not appear to be taking it too easy*'. To be sure, much opposition to emigration was sincere, and many of post-famine Ireland's most prominent men had themselves spent time abroad, witnessed emigrant poverty, and returned home determined to oppose the exodus. Nevertheless, bishop Butler's private remark, made in response to Fenian attempts to capitalize on lower-class discontent, revealed profound ambiguity in the nationalist position. Bourgeois nationalists had to address emigration and its socioeconomic causes because those issues, rather than political abstractions such as home rule, were the ones which most concerned the disadvantaged elements of Ireland society whose mass support the nationalists wanted and needed. Thus, grass-roots pressures forced nationalists to link the political goals of the middle class to the practical grievances and aspirations of the masses – more specifically, to promises of fundamental socioeconomic changes which would obviate the need for mass emigration.

By all accounts, nationalists were successful in forging that link, as historians' studies indicate that nationalism's fiercest partisans were members of precisely those groups most threatened by economic displacement and the necessity of emigration. However, the social issues which mobilized landless labourers, farmers' noninheriting sons, and urban workers were potentially dangerous, for if thwarted in their material aspirations by their middle-class leaders' concessions to British authority or to indigenous bourgeois interests, those men might either disrupt nationalist unity (e.g., by attacking middle-class 'patriots') or switch allegiance to more extreme varieties of nationalism, as during the 1922-23 civil war. Cognisant of these dangers, nationalist leaders were of two minds on emigration, since mass departures by the dispossessed and discontented would vitiate nationalist movements, whereas their presence in Ireland might disrupt or divert those movements into unacceptable channels. The dilemma was clearly stated during the Anglo-Irish war when the Dáil's defence minister urged Ireland's sons to 'stand fast', while its minister of agriculture warned that, if they did, in their land-hunger they would 'swarm . . . onto the land' belonging to graziers and strong farmers, thus alienating both the bourgeoisie and the church from the national struggle.

The source of this dilemma was that most Catholic leaders, bourgeois products of an increasingly capitalist society, had little or no inclination to take the really radical measures necessary to restructure that society and so halt emigration. These men had risen to the top of an Irish Catholic society whose very shape and stability depended to a large degree on emigration's continuance; indeed, their very affluence and authority derived from existing socioeconomic structures and institutions which could not flourish or perhaps even survive if emigration ceased. As a result, with very few exceptions such as Michael Davitt and James Connolly, once they had achieved national prominence no post-famine political leaders advocated, much less implemented, measures sufficient to stop emigration. Thus, in the face of grazier opposition, Parnell retreated from his suggestion that western smallholders colonize the north Leinster grasslands, and after 1921 Arthur Griffith's lieutenants eschewed the protective tariffs which he had urged to create industrial employment. Likewise, on local levels nationalist leaders were financially dependent on, when they were not synonymous with, Catholic Ireland's entrenched interests: middle-class farmers and townsmen who were staunchly opposed to land redistribution, land nationalization, socialism – often even to cooperative enterprises and tariffs – in short, to any fundamental changes in a social system which had permanently institutionalized lower-class emigration.

Emigration and the Myth of Holy Ireland

Caught between their poor followers' demands that they support radical measures to halt emigration, and their affluent adherents' and their own aversion to such steps, bourgeois nationalists and churchmen had to formulate 'explanations' of emigration in ideological contexts which would ignore or obscure post-famine Ireland's social realities and conflicts. As a result, their interpretations of emigration were integrally related to their idealization of a semimythical 'holy Ireland' which could be defended against both external assault and internal schism. Although this ideal emerged vaguely in the early 19th century, after the famine it sharpened and assumed a profoundly antimodernist thrust as the papacy's contemporary crusade against secularism, coupled with the sentimental romanticism pervading bourgeois culture, only reinforced Irish leaders' increasingly strident rhetorical reactions against 'British' influences. In response, they conceptualized a fortress Hibernia, an ideal and purportedly 'traditional' Catholic Ireland which was antithetical to their images of England and America and to the 'modern' and allegedly 'alien' tendencies within Ireland itself. Thus, according to Catholic leaders, especially churchmen, Irish Catholics were superior to the English and to all Protestants because of their relative indifference to material wealth and to the false gods of urban-industrial civilization. Because of such unworldliness, allegedly the Irish were profoundly conservative, content to live simple lives at home under clerical guidance and in harmony with family, neighbours, and natural environment. Similarly, the ideal Irish society for such folk was static, organic, and paternalistic – a divinely-ordained hierarchy devoid of internal conflicts, insulated by faith from potential 'contamination'. To ensure such stability and continuity, 'holy Ireland's' economy needed to remain overwhelmingly agricultural, based on the peasant family – the devout and paternal microcosm of the larger society. To be sure, lay and clerical nationalists played variations on these common themes,[4] but all save a few social radicals conceptualized an ideally-unchanging social order which, in theory, could support all Ireland's people in frugal comfort. Sometimes their rhetoric implied that this model society was still in the process of creation, at other times indicated that it was already in being. However, in either case its perceived enemies

– landlordism, Protestantism, secularism, socialism – were legion, and so 'holy Ireland' needed constant and vigorous defence: hence, the church's assiduous efforts to shape Catholic minds by controlling education; its support for home rule as a means to insulate the faithful from pernicious English legislation and 'anglicizing' influences; and, despite the bishops' usual concern for property rights, its espousal of agrarian reforms designed to root the 'peasantry' in the soil and so secure 'holy Ireland's' social and moral foundation.

Within this conceptual framework, clerics and nationalists could both oppose emigration and condemn the emigrants themselves. For although the notion of a divinely-ordered Irish society could reinforce churchmen's sometime boast that its pious emigrants were furthering God's work overseas, the more prevalent imagery of 'holy Ireland' struggling against the forces of evil implied that mass departures constituted an intolerable weakening of its ranks. In addition, the very ideal of 'holy Ireland' made emigration seem highly inappropriate, if not treacherous. If, as many Catholic spokesmen claimed by the 1890s, the ideal Irish society was already in being, then continued emigration indicated that subtle, subversive forces were at work internally. Since Catholic leaders already had created most or all of the conditions and institutions which purportedly obviated emigration's further necessity, then by the logic of their vision any departures which still occurred implied the emigrants' self-willed or self-deluded repudiation of the organic nation-as-family and their violation of the sacralized 'peasant' ethos on which the nation was supposedly based. After all, even if America still offered superior material advantages (which many Catholic spokesmen were no longer willing to admit), Irish Catholics by definition were supposedly too selfless and unworldly to succumb to such lures. Hence, the emigrants must be either 'traitors' or 'fools'; indeed, Patrick Pearse stigmatized them as both.

Of course, the ideology of 'holy Ireland' imperfectly reflected only the residual, traditional aspects of post-famine society's complex realities, and in the sense that it ignored, obscured, or denied the real and often ruthless effects of capitalist development, the concept was at best an appealing self-delusion, at worst a pious fraud. Not only did those who propagated the image fail to use their influence to make reality match the dream of an organic society capable of sustaining all its people, but even conceptually the notion of 'holy Ireland' was grievously flawed with respect to emigration. In a sense, it was merely a rhetorical cloak, woven of medieval dogmas and Victorian pieties, masking a petty bourgeois society whose vaunted stability and sacralized family farm both mandated and depended on constant emigration by the disinherited and dispossessed. Furthermore, the concept not only ignored Irish Protestants, but failed to make any concession to the need for Irish cities and industries as outlets for the countryside's surplus population: Ireland must remain rural, churchmen demanded, for urbanization and industrialization connoted secularism, social fragmentation, and the 'black devil of Socialism'. In the light of these anomalies, Catholic spokesmen's demands that emigrants not desert 'the holy peace of home' for the fleshpots of America smacked of wilful blindness, if not gross hypocrisy.

Moreover, the ideological problem remained. If the agrarian-capitalist realities behind the 'holy Ireland' mask were the real causes of emigration, how could the spokesmen for the Catholic bourgeoisie explain continuing mass departures without dropping the mask and revealing both their community's social inequities and their own practical infidelity to the organic ideal – and without thereby alienating the emigrants from their leadership and from the society left behind? To be sure, nationalists and clerics could redouble their denunciations of the emigrants as 'fools' and 'traitors', but such epithets violated realities too grossly and threatened to embitter the emigrants toward 'holy Ireland' and its guardians. Or, they could resort to the old religious rationalization 'that God in his inscrutable wisdom . . . had intended and used the Irish race to carry Catholicism to the ends of the earth', but, as one trenchant critic perceived, 'the Irishman who accepts this teaching cannot any longer lay the misfortunes of his country upon the shoulders of the British government'. Thus, the most logical and prevalent recourse was to fall back on the oldest 'explanation' of all, that emigration was 'exile' forced by British oppression. That interpretation implied no criticism of 'holy Ireland', but postponed embarrassing social questions until after independence was won – and in the meantime, Catholic Ireland's apologists hoped, it would deflect the emigrants' 'fierce rage and fury' against the British 'misgovernment' which obliged emigration from 'a land capable of supporting twice its present population'. Nor did that interpretation imply criticism of the emigrants themselves, for they were merely 'victims' whose assiduously-cultivated love for their homeland and hatred for England would inspire their unceasing devotion and donations to 'holy Ireland's' staunch defenders – the Catholic clergy and Irish and Irish-American nationalists.

Conclusion

To be sure, Irish socialist James Connolly and a few others voiced dissent from both the dominant ideology and its facile 'explanations' of emigration, and many emigrants themselves were too realistic or alienated to conceptualize their departures in prescribed ways. Nevertheless, the flood of remittances and donations alone indicates that most Catholic emigrants adhered to the exile motif and remained emotionally or at least publicly loyal to the society which had expelled them. In part, this was because the concept of emigration as exile was both deeply rooted in Irish traditions and constantly reinforced by contemporary conflicts with landlords, Orangemen, and British officials, thus corroborating 'official' Catholic rhetoric. However, since the fundamental causes of most post-famine emigration stemmed from the structures and dynamics of Catholic society itself, it is doubtful whether the notion of emigration as exile would have retained such popularity had the exile motif and the 'holy Ireland' concept not been natural and logical expressions of a still-prevalent, traditional worldview which condemned innovation and individualism while externalizing responsibility for unsettling change. Not only did 'holy Ireland' seem to be at least a partly valid metaphor for a society still largely centred on family farm and parish church, but, even more crucially, it was a systematic expression of what a people in rapid social and cultural transition desperately wanted and needed to believe was still entirely true about their society and themselves. Thus, emigration as exile's basic appeal lay in its symbolic resolution of the discrepancies between the reality of social fragmentation and the ideal of organic community. After all, if England could yet be blamed for emigration's causes, for the inability of 'holy Ireland' to support all her children, then both the emigrants and those who profited by their departures could be absolved of culpability, while the consequent resentments against England could themselves reinforce the outlooks and allegiances which held Catholic Ireland together in the face of the disintegrative and potentially demoralizing effects of commercialization and anglicization.

Thus, the traditions of the Catholic masses, their needs for continuity and reassurance, and the hegemonic imperatives of Catholic clergymen and nationalist politicians converged to control and obscure the real conflicts and discontinuities within Catholic society. So, when in 1887 a traveller asked a farm labourer in Tipperary whether his exploited fellow workers subscribed to the bourgeois-defined and -led home rule movement, the man replied that although '[t]hey hate the farmers, . . . *they love Ireland, and they all stand together for the counthry'*. And, mystified by an imagery which both mitigated and externalized their resentments, such men usually blamed England when they left home seeking the dignity and decent wages denied them by the 'pathriotic' graziers and shopkeepers of 'holy Ireland'.

Postscript[5]
Although the experience of the Irish Free State belied the promise that political independence alone would halt emigration, at least until after World War II it appears that most Catholic Irish still adhered to the dominant ideology and blamed the continued exodus on the legacies of British rule, particularly on 'the border'. However, the great postwar surge in emigration (primarily to England) shattered complacency, and in the 1950s and, especially, the 1960s the Dublin government abandoned Griffith's and de Valera's dream of 'capitalism in one country' and embraced new economic policies which brought about dramatic growth and a temporary cessation of emigration. As a result, Irish society has become far more affluent and somewhat less provincial than ever before, but also more urbanized, secularized, and socially and culturally fragmented. Traditional outlooks and identities once bound up with unquestioning allegiances to family, church, and orthodox nationalism have eroded and become confused or conditional, and a once

relatively homogeneous 'holy Ireland' has become a diverse 'consumer society'.

Nevertheless, during the last decade a faltering and, perhaps, fatally flawed 'modernization' has created unprecedented social dislocation and division, soaring unemployment and crime rates, and new pressures for mass emigration. To date, political and clerical responses to the new wave of departures have been surprisingly muted, especially in contrast to the anguished protests voiced in the post-famine era. Some spokesmen have voiced concern over the 'brain drain' of young, well-educated technocrats, less so for the plight of poor and unskilled migrants, while others have quietly or, in a few cases, openly recognized the expediency of a new safety valve to siphon off the revolutionary potential of the disillusioned and disadvantaged. However, in either case an embracing ideology (such as 'holy Ireland') which could oppose emigration, however superficially, seems to exist no longer among the nation's 'modernizing elite'. Perhaps their conscious role since 1960 in inviting British (and other foreign) capital to recolonize Ireland, plus their fear of encouraging popular support for the Provos' atavistic and now inconvenient nationalism, dissuades today's Catholic leaders from blaming England for emigration or its causes. More broadly, their embrace of international capitalism and its concomitant values inevitably implies acceptance of both the necessity and desirability of untrammelled labour mobility and the inefficacy or undesirability of comprehensive political solutions which would violate the reigning 'free market' ethos.

Indeed, to the degree that that ethos now permeates all Irish social strata, mass emigration may constitute no fundamental threat to the new socioeconomic and political order. Many of today's prospective emigrants seem to welcome emigration as individual opportunity. Or, if prevented from leaving Ireland by legal restrictions overseas, some merely turn to various forms of criminal but emulative consumerism, rather than to new political solutions based on radical notions of organic community. Likewise, although the recent Ballinspittle phenomenon suggests that many Irish youths still yearn for traditional religious solutions to contemporary social crises, the reactionary responses by the church and some sectors of the bourgeoisie to advanced capitalism's logical side-effects (marital breakdown, 'sexual permissiveness') merely corroborate rather than challenge the parameters of the established social order and – like the 'holy Ireland' ideal – provide only the illusion of continuity with a vanished past.

Long ago, James Connolly wrote that it was an outrage for an Irishman to 'rear his child up to love its country' while 'supporting a social system which declares that the child has no right to the country, but must pay for permission to live on it as it is the property of private individuals' and corporations. In Ireland today it is questionable whether either the privileged or the poor are still capable of such indignation, much less of the imagination and will to act upon it. To be sure, once abroad many contemporary emigrants become disillusioned and resentful; no longer channelled against 'British tyranny', their anger and unhappiness are often directed against Ireland's political establishment. However, the emigrants' new perspectives cannot upset the socioeconomic and political consensus prevailing in Dublin, for the Irish government is conveniently unique among western European nations in its refusal to allow its citizens overseas the opportunity to vote in domestic elections. Ironically, the leaders of a nation whose very creation once depended on the politicization of emigrant grief now seem to fear that its newest generation of 'banished children' might finally apprehend the real reasons for its and its predecessors' 'exile'.

Footnotes

1. All but the 'Postscript' of this essay represents an abbreviated version of material which appears in my book, *Emigrants and Exiles: Ireland and the Irish Exodus to North America* (New York: Oxford University Press, 1985), especially pp. 102-130 and 427-492. Material in this essay also appeared in *Studies* Winter 1988.

2. For example, it was symptomatic that few post-famine emigrants financed the transatlantic passage from their own earnings or capital, as was the case earlier; rather, most were totally dependent on the initiative and largesse of relatives at home or, most often, abroad, a situation which probably encouraged the retention of passive, non-responsible attitudes.

3. See Miller, *Emigrants and Exiles*, pp. 481-492.

4. For example, nationalist politicians regarded the home rule movement or, later, Sinn Féin as coguardians with the church of the people's traditions, and Parnell hoped that a patriotic landlord class might play a guiding role. Likewise, urban-

oriented nationalists such as Arthur Griffith envisioned a partnership between agriculture and industry, while Gaelic leaders desired the idealized peasant-citizen to be Irish-speaking as well as pious. However, similarities of vision outweighed the differences.

5. This part of the essay is based on an unpublished paper which I delivered to a seminar at the College of Industrial Relations, Dublin, in spring, 1986: 'Prosperity, depression and Irish emigration: a comparison, 1780-1844 and 1960-86'. The disillusion and resentment of contemporary Irish emigrants in America is recorded in nearly every issue of the New York *Irish Voice*.

The Fifth Province: Between the Global and the Local

RICHARD KEARNEY

When we speak of the Irish community today, we mean not only the national community but also our international communities abroad and our subnational communities at home. This Irish triangle has been translated into a French one by George Quigley who refers to a benign *ménage à trois* where the global, national and regional levels of community might happily co-habit. But whatever one's linguistic or geometrical preference, one thing is clear: the Irish sense of belonging is no longer predetermined by the map-lines of our island. *Beyond* those frontiers extend emigré populations of over seventy million people who claim Irish descent. While *within* those frontiers, we have four provincial regions (one of which is our troubled Ulster) which, in turn, divide into a multiplicity of local communities.

Are we then condemned to futile fragmentation? Or is it not possible that a revised and more enabling sense of ourselves may emerge from such definitions; is it perhaps at the crossroads where the local and global communities overlap that we may rediscover the the 'fifth province' of the ancient Irish imagination – of which it has been written:

Modern Ireland is made up of four provinces. And yet, the Irish word for a province is *coiced* which means a fifth. This fivefold division is as old as Ireland itself, yet there is disagreement about the identity of the fifth. Some claim that all the provinces met at the Stone of Divisions on the Hill of Uisneach, believed to be the mid-point of Ireland. Others say that the fifth province was Meath (Mide), the 'middle'. Both

109

traditions divide Ireland into four quarters and a 'middle', though they disagree about the location of this middle or 'fifth' province. Although Tara was the political centre of Ireland, this fifth province acted as a second centre, which although non-political, was just as important, acting as a necessary balance. The present unhappy state of our country would seem to indicate a need for this second centre of gravity. The obvious impotence of the various political attempts to unite the four geographical provinces would seem to warrant another kind of solution, another kind of unity, one which would incorporate the 'fifth' province. This province, this place, this centre, is not a political or geographical position, it is more like a disposition. What kind of place could this be? (Editorial, *The Crane Bag*, Vol. I, No. 1, 1977).

My wager here is that this place is not a fixed point but a set of relations extending from the participatory democracy of the local communities at home to the disseminated migrations of the Irish communities abroad. The 'fifth province' is to be found, if anywhere, at the swinging door which connects the global with the local. The answer to the old proverb: 'where is the middle of the world' remains as true as ever – 'here and elsewhere'.

I

A few words first about the global dimension. The internationalization of the Irish community is not only a matter of the extended Irish family abroad. It also bears on our political and cultural understanding of ourselves as an island nation. Being surrounded by water can be seen either as an insulating device against alien influences or as an open exchange with other peoples and places (as it was traditionally celebrated in our maritime literature, which spoke of the constant coming and going between Ireland and the wider world). The ancient Irish voyage tales or *Immrama* – from *Mael Duin* to the *Navigatio Brendani* – record the migrations of Irish men of learning to the Continent and the New World in search of the Isles of the Blessed (another name for the Fifth Province?). While our cultural memory has registered the multiple *navigatios* of our great thinkers – Eriugena, Columbanus, Berkeley, Toland, Burke – to foreign shores and back again. Our travelling artists tell a similar story, from Wilde and Joyce to Beckett and Le Brocquy.

Nor should we forget the creative expressions of those migrant Irish minds engaged in the more popular and contemporary media of music and cinema. I am thinking in particular of recent statements by U2's Bono and film-maker Neil Jordan in their contributions to *Across the Frontiers* (1989). 'Maybe we Irish are misfits', as Bono put it, 'travellers, never really at home, but always talking about it . . . we're like salmon: it's upriver all the time, against the odds, the river doesn't want us . . . yet we want a way home'. Or as Jordan observed: 'The great stupidity of Irish history has been the pretence to be a self-enclosed and uncon-fused nation . . . Our mistake was to believe that we could be at home in a single nation . . . We thus forgot that we can never be at home anywhere. Perhaps it is the function of the writer to remind the nation of this: to expose the old ideologies. To feel in exile abroad and also when one returns home'. Prefacing these remarks by Bono and Jordan, I commented: 'The Irish thing surfaces, sometimes in spite of itself, when the obsession with an exclusive identity is abandoned. The reason we could not find it was perhaps that we were looking too hard, too self-consciously, too fanatically. Now, as we are rediscovering ourselves through our encounters with others, reclaiming our voice in our migra-tions through other cultures and continents – Europe, Britain, North America – we are beginning to realize that the Irish thing was always there. We could not recognize it for as long as we assumed we were at home with ourselves, sufficient unto our-selves, slaves to the illusion that we were masters of a land apart, Robinson Crusoes on our sequestered island. It takes the migrant mind to know that the island is without frontiers, that the seas are waterways connecting us with others, that the journey to the other place harbours the truth of homecoming to our own place'. (*Across the Frontiers*, Wolfhound Press 1989, p. 187)

Is the interconnectedness of Irish and non-Irish cultures not evident in the manner in which some of our most talented contemporary artists blend together national and international idioms? Do not poets such as Heaney, Mahon, Longley or McGuckian demonstrate how indigenous material can be combined with the most innovative forms of international literature? Do not painters such as Le Brocquy, Ballagh, Mulcahy and Madden, or musicians such as the Chieftains, Van Morrison, Enya and U2, show how one can draw inspiration from Irish sources while also communicating with the citizens of other cultures? And do not film makers such as Jordan, Murphy, Sheridan, O'Connor and Comerford testify to the fact that images drawn from one's native society can be displayed and appreciated throughout the capitals of the world? Maybe this is what Joyce had in mind when he embarked on the imaginative project of 'hibernicizing Europe and Europeanising Ireland'.

This interpenetration of Irish and world cultures applies not only at the level of art but also at the level of communications. Ireland's increasing participation in the transnational satellite communications system is a decisive instance of this. By the mid 1990s the new communications technology will have connected Ireland to European and global media networks. This movement towards a more integrated and interconnected audiovisual culture is well underway. The recent launching of two European Satellite Stations – LA SEPT by the French and SAT 3 by the Germans – to promote cultural unity-in-diversity is already having a significant impact on co-productions across national boundaries; while the European Space Agency Satellites are currently equipped to link up information centres throughout the European community, and beyond. Whether these advances in communications technology produce a society of 'misunderstanding minds' (to borrow Joyce's phrase) or 'inter-understanding minds', remains to be seen. But one thing is clear: Shem the Penman (the Joycean man of letters) can no longer be separated from Shaun the Postman (the man of communications). The globalization of Irish culture is also a mediatization –for better or for worse. The challenge is, of course, to make it better rather than worse.

Finally, no discussion of the current internationalizing of Ireland can ignore recent political decisions with regard to the old chestnut of national sovereignty. The most significant date here is undoubtedly 1992, which heralds the culmination of the movement towards an integrated Europe of 220 million people, as agreed by the twelve member states with the signing of the Single European Act in 1988. But this readiness to cede or share sovereignty did not begin, for Ireland, with the ratification of the SEA. It has been a gradual process going back at least as far as the famous communiqué issued after the December 1980 Anglo-Irish Summit, which referred to the potential resolution of the Anglo-Irish problem – i.e. Ulster – within the terms of a new 'totality of relationships'. The Forum for a New Ireland, to which all Irish constitutional nationalist parties contributed between 1980 and 1984, specified these terms of reference to include the option of joint-authority (i.e. Irish and British) in Northern Ireland. And the final Anglo-Irish Agreement of 1985, while not going as far as joint-authority, did nonetheless represent a significant step toward the future pooling of sovereignties between the two islands: a process which, with the passing of the SEA in 1988, extends the 'totality of relations' beyond Ireland and Britain to include the other member states of the EC. And why should it stop there? Do not recent moves to bring down the barriers separating Eastern and Western Europe, together with Gorbachev's repeated appeals to a 'common house of Europe', not offer the hope that we may soon see the realization of De Gaulle's vision of a Europe extending from the Atlantic to the Urals?

What I am basically observing is that Irish culture and politics can no longer be contained within the frontiers of an island. And what I am submitting is that this may signal a movement beyond the historical alternatives of colonial dependence and nationalist independence towards a new model of post-colonial and post-nationalist interdependence. If Germany and France were able to overcome their 'national rivalries', which had caused two world wars in our century, and forge the Monet-Schumann alliance which eventually issued in the European Community as we know it, why not Ireland and Britain? If Mitterand and Kohl could meet at Verdun and shake hands across their national borders, why not Thatcher and Haughey, Paisley and Hume? Is it not significant that Irish MEPs from the North and the South, from the Unionist and Nationalist communities, can vote together on matters of mutual interest in Strasbourg and Brussels while they remain at loggerheads within their own national territories?

I think there is a growing recognition of this amongst the politicians and intellectuals of these islands. Leaders as different as Haughey and Thatcher, Hume and Molyneux have invoked the idea of an extended 'totality of relationships' in a positive fashion – recognising both its Anglo-Irish and European implications. These are spelled out in explicit form in John Hume's recent call for a 'new republicanism':

> The real new republicanism is the development of processes which will allow people to preserve their culture, rights and dignity; to promote their well-being and have a means of controlling the forces which will affect their lives . . . this will allow us better to fulfil our potential as a people; to contribute to our world; to rediscover the cultural interaction between Ireland and Europe; to reinvolve ourselves in political relationships with those on the Continental mainland and to enjoy properly the inchoate European outlook and vision which was lost in our oppressive and obsessive relationship with Britain. It maintains the necessary synchrony between the scope of democracy and economic and technological circumstances . . . On this basis we can provide a social, regional and Irish dimension to our Europe (*Across the Frontiers – Ireland in the 1990s*, p. 56).

Roy Foster also gestures towards a reappraisal of our traditional understanding of national sovereignty when he speaks of the need to broaden our definitions of 'nationalism, making it inclusive rather than exclusive. 'The very notion of indivisible sovereignty is now being questioned', he observes, and 'the concepts of dual allegiance and cultural diversity are surely associated'. Foster clarifies his searching position with the following bold statement: 'Cultural self-confidence can exist without being yoked to a determinist and ideologically redundant notion of unilaterally-declared nation-statehood; political and cultural credentials have for too long been identified together' ('Varieties of Irishness' in *Cultural Traditions in Northern Ireland*, 1989, p. 20).

It may well be the case that, by the 1990s, inhabitants of this island will enjoy a triple citizenship of Ireland, Europe and the world.

II

Does not this accelerating movement towards a more *global* understanding of community not call for a counter-balancing movement towards a renewed sense of *local* belonging? Does a new sense of internationalism not need to be complemented by a strong and countervailing commitment to regionalism? The idea of a transnational democracy is meaningless without the reality of participatory democracy at the level of local community. That, at any rate, is the thesis I wish to pursue in this second part of my paper. Without this commitment to local democracy there is a danger that we would merely be replacing the old British model of Empire with a new super-state imperialism at the European or Atlantic level.

What I offer here are some general reflections on the philosophy of community – bearing in mind the mischievously ambiguous remark made to me at a recent conference by the historian, Marianne Elliott: 'You philosophers are so lucky. You can say anything and get away with it. You never have to quote sources, because you don't have any!'

In all societies with representative governments, power supposedly resides in the people. This means, in turn, that the people empower certain elected individuals to represent them in parliament, to act in their name and on their behalf. When we talk of the loss of confidence in a governing power, this signifies that the people are withdrawing their consent from their representatives.

In order to maintain the system, those in power often begin to act as sovereign rulers, as monarchs; they substitute force for the assent of the people (*demos*). They try to fill the 'credibility gap' by charisma or coercion.

Another way of trying to resolve this crisis of consent is to foment an internal sense of national solidarity by identifying a common external enemy. Hence the use of the Falklands factor in Thatcherite Britain; the reds under the beds syndrome in McCarthyite America; the witch-hunt of so-called 'foreign-backed' counter-revolutionaries in contemporary China. But scapegoating of this kind does not work in the long run – for the scapegoaters know, though they may seek to hide it from themselves, that those scapegoated are not *really* what they are denounced as being: the Jews did not really poison the wells or ruin the economy; the Reds did not really infiltrate the apparatus of national security and communications; the 'Argies' were not really a threat to British identity and sovereignty; the student leaders in Tienenman Square were not really spies in the payroll of Western capitalists. And so on. Scapegoating can never ultimately succeed as a solution to the crisis of national insecurity and fragmentation for it is always based, as Sartre reminds us, on 'bad faith'. You cannot go on believing forever in your own lies. Self-deception is a shaky basis for self-confidence.

Irresolvable conflicts between sovereign nation-states lead ultimately to war. As Hannah Arendt argues in *Crises of the Republic* (1972): 'So long as *national independence*, namely freedom from foreign rule, and the *sovereignty of the state*, namely the claim to unchecked and unlimited power in foreign affairs, are equated . . . not even a theoretical solution of the problem of war is conceivable, and a guaranteed peace on earth is as utopian as the squaring of the circle'. And she adds: 'What we call the *state* is not much older than the sixteenth century and the same is true of the concept of *sovereignty*. Sovereignty means, among other things, that conflicts of an international character can ultimately be settled only by war; there is no other last resort' (p. 229).

Since war is clearly unacceptable as a resort – last or otherwise – for the resolution of conflicts between sovereign states, an alternative concept of government is called for. Arendt suggests a federal model where power would operate horizontally rather than vertically: the federated units – e.g. councils or communities – mutually checking and controlling each other's powers.

One has to be careful here, however, to distinguish between a super-national federation and a genuinely inter-national one. The danger of the former is that it can easily be monopolized by the nation that happens to be the strongest – thus leading to the tyranny of a single global government (or police force) from which there would be no escape. A properly and equitably *inter-*national system, by contrast, would be one which draws its authority not from above but from below – from the genuine participatory democracy of local community councils.

The most realistic alternative to the state or superstate system of centralized authority is, I believe, a federated community of communities – and preferably one founded on the council system. Everytime it has emerged in history, the council system has been destroyed by party or state bureaucracy. This is true of the French Revolution, the American Revolution (as pioneered by Jefferson), the Parisian Commune, the original Russian Soviets, the German and Austrian revolutions at the end of the first world war, and the Hungarian revolution in the fifties. In each of these instances, the council system emerged spontaneously as a direct response to the requirements of democratic political action. They grew from the real experience of local participatory democracy. A council system of this kind, to which the principle of absolute sovereignty would be totally alien, is perfectly suited to the possibility of an inter-national federation. And the fact that it *has* not yet been realized does not mean that it *will* not. The very reminder of how many times it has been ardently promoted in times of historical inventiveness is itself a signal of hope that some day the conditions will indeed be right and the democratic readiness to achieve it present. The recent experiments with Civic Forum models in Eastern Europe augur well.

In the meantime, we might ask if there are any specifically Irish precedents for such a participatory form of social and cultural democracy.

I believe that the Vandaleur communities in Ralahine and the rural co-operative movement inaugurated by George Russell (AE) and Horace Plunkett toward the close of the last century, were just such experiments in local democracy. The cooperative project for self-determination at community level was an extraordinary venture in decentralized decision-making and one which should be written into our history books and, indeed, into a revised Irish Constitution.

But is such a vision of local democratic communities a dead letter in Ireland today? The contemporary troubles in Northern Ireland have compelled several political minds, north and south of the border, to consider the possibility of decentralizing power from the state to regional and local authorities. Following the lead of France, Holland and Denmark – whose growth in the domestic provision of local authorities has corresponded to a rise in economic growth – Irish intellectuals as diverse as John Hume, the late Sean MacBride, Michael D. Higgins, Edna Longley and Tom Barrington have argued for new models of regional government.

At the launching of the Northern Issue of the *Crane Bag* on December 9, 1980 – just one day after the historic Anglo-Irish communiqué on the new 'totality of relationships' – Sean MacBride issued the following plea for local democracy in a federated Ireland. 'The unitary state is not the only option', he declared. 'The time has come to take another look at our system of government and to recognize the wisdom of a decentralized Irish federation of counties (as first proposed by Alfred O'Rahilly in the thirties). Do we want centralized bureaucracy? Would we not be better off with four regional or even 32 local parliaments? There could be an overall coordinating body which if it was like the Swiss central government would be like a board of directors, proportionately representing all parties. But each canton would remain in control of its own decision-making'.

To prevent such local councils falling into the trap of local chauvinism – or what Kavanagh termed 'provincialism' – it would be necessary, of course, to ensure a supervisory role for international committees such as Amnesty or the European Court to protect the rights of minority groups, and the individuals within each group. In the absence of such a universal court of appeal, the devolution of power to self-governing communities could easily degenerate into a myriad of insular communes where the local chieftain could lord it over any dissenters, unchallenged and unchecked. Without the guarantee of some international tribunal of arbitration, one might simply end up replacing the collective intolerance of states and super-states with the particular, and often more soul-destroying, intolerance of the neighbourhood. The valley of squinting windows syndrome.

That is why the most likely model of regional democracy to succeed in Ireland, at the present historical juncture, is one brought about within the context of an integrated Europe of equal regions. This is what John Hume proposed in his *Report on Regional Policy*, drafted in July 1987, and unanimously approved by the European Parliament in October 1987. What the continuing debate on the new Europe of Regions brings home to us, again and again, is that if regional power without European integration runs the risk of neo-tribalism, an integrated Europe without devolution to the regions runs the risk of neo-imperialism. Both extremes are equally undesirable, and equally avoidable if the proper balance betwen inter-national and sub-national government can be struck.

The project of local participatory democracy demands a unique blend of cultural inventiveness and political commitment. It ignites that sense of excitement people experience when they discover they are the creators of their own lives; that institutions and constitutions are of their own making; that the future is an open horizon. As Yeats observed, when 'people are trying to found a new society, politicians want to be artistic and artistic people to be political'.

*　　*　　*

Before concluding, I would like to cite the example of two Northern Irish poets – John Hewitt and Seamus Heaney – who have responded to the political and cultural traumas of their native province by devoting their imaginative energies to a sense of region that is at once specific and universal, lived and aspired after.

Already in the forties, Hewitt, a native of Ulster and curator of the Ulster Museum, acknowledged regionalism as a way of resolving and responding to the seemingly incorrigible conflict of identities in Northern Ireland. In *The Bitter Gourd* (1947) he wrote with customary percipience: 'To return for only a moment to this question of "rootedness". I do not mean that a writer ought to live and die in the house of his fathers. What I do mean is that he ought to feel that he belongs to a recognisable focus in place and time. How he assures himself of that feeling is his own affair. But I believe he must have it. And with it, he must have ancestors. Not just of the blood, but of the emotions, of the quality and *slant* of mind. He must know where he comes from and where he is: otherwise how can he tell where he wishes to go?' Two years later in a publication entitled *Regionalism: The Last Chance* (1947), Hewitt turns his attention to some of the larger political implcations of regional identity. And most significantly, I believe, he fully recognizes the necessity for regional fidelities to remain open to a universal dimension. 'Ulster considered as a Region', he writes here, 'and not as the symbol of any particular creed, can command the loyalty of every one of its inhabitants. For Regional identity does not preclude, rather it requires, membership of a larger association. And whatever that association be . . . there should emerge a culture and an attitude individual and distinctive, a fine contribution to the European inheritance and no mere echo of the thought and imagination of another people or another land'. The second Hewitt International Summer School, held in County Antrim in August 1989, was dedicated appropriately to the exploration of a cultural and political regionalism dear to Hewitt himself.

Seamus Heaney elaborates on the idea of regional identity in an essay entitled 'The Sense of Place', first delivered as a lecture in the Ulster Museum in 1977 and later published in his collection of prose essays, *Preoccupations* (1980). Taking his tune from Kavanagh's poem 'Epic', which compares a local skirmish between Duffys and McCabes with the 'bother' caused by the *Putsch* in Munich, Heaney explains how in this poem – as presumably in most good poetry – 'the local idiom extends beyond the locale itself'. More exactly: 'Munich, the European theatre, is translated into the local speech to become bother, and once it is bother, it has become knowable, and no more splendid than the bother at home. Language, as well as gods, makes its own importance – the sense of place issues in a point of view, a phrase that Kavanagh set great store by and used always as a positive. He cherished the ordinary, the actual, the known, the unimportant'. So does Heaney. And one feels he is also partial to Kavanagh's view, cited later in the lecture, that 'parochialism is universal'.

But Heaney is also aware that forty odd years have passed between Kavanagh's poem and his own lecture. The sense of belonging to a more enlarged space is incontrovertible, even if it does not diminish the search for one's own place. 'We are no longer innocent', he concludes, 'we are no longer just parishioners of the local. We go to Paris at Easter instead of rolling eggs on the hill at the gable. "Chicken Marengo! – it's a far cry from the Moy", Paul Muldoon says in a line depth-charged with architectural history. Yet those primary laws of our nature are still operative. We are dwellers, we are namers, we are lovers, we make homes and search for our histories'.

The fact that Hewitt hails from Protestant Planter stock and Heaney from Catholic Nationalist, is revealing to the extent that both find common ground in an Ulster regional identity (Hewitt's Antrim, Heaney's Derry) interconnected with the larger world. Both gravitate toward a 'bottomless centre' bespoken to a more global circumference.

Concluding Note

A wise man once remarked that a field was never ploughed by turning it over in the mind. I suspect, however, that if it wasn't turned in the mind first, there never would have been a ploughed field at all. In any case, I would like to conclude now with a short list of some of the most conspicuous experiments in participatory regional democracy in Ireland today. There is the North Centre City Action Project in Dublin and the Development Scheme in Shannon, both of which have managed to combine financial support at international level with the dynamic energies and resources of the local region. There is also the Ros a 'Mhíl project in County Galway where the local community succeeded in securing monies from the European Structural and Regional Funds to construct a new pier for fishing and sea-transport, thereby forging a promising economic future for themselves. And one might also mention the North West Project and Waterside Projects in Derry, run respectively by two community leaders, Paddy Doherty and Glen Barr, drawing simultaneously from grass-roots community involvement and youth employment schemes grant-aided by the internationally-based Ireland Funds and European Funds. (Indeed, the North West Project has been so successful that it is now the highest employer in Derry with Dupont.) Finally, one could cite the recent success of community cultural projects such as CAFE (Creative Arts for Everyone) or City Centre in Dublin, which operate on a partnership basis of international support (Ireland Funds, Gulbenkian Foundation, Yamaha) and Arts Council subsidies in order to assist the local community in the creation and organization of its own culture.

Empowering our local communities to develop a sense of self-confidence and self-discovery is, I believe, one of the best contributions we can make to the global community. It points in the direction of a regional pluralism capable of cultivating, in Roy Foster's phrase, 'an affirmation of differences which might lead to mutual acceptance' ('Varieties of Irishness', p. 21). This linking of the local and the global is arguably the most promising formula for a regenerated sense of Irish community. Following the lead of those community cultural groups which have managed to creatively express their sense of local identity at the same time as they transcend both tribal and national boundaries, we may eventually realize the truth of Coventry Patmore's hope – often cited by Seamus Heaney – that the 'end of art is peace'.

Some books from
WOLFHOUND PRESS
write for our current catalogue to
68 MOUNTJOY SQUARE · DUBLIN 1

ACROSS THE FRONTIERS: Ireland in the 1990s
Cultural, Political, Economic
Edited by RICHARD KEARNEY
280 pages · 216x138mm ISBN 0 86327 209 6 HB

Leading Irish and European intellectuals, politicians and artists provide stimulating, innovative analyses of Ireland's cultural, political and economic relationships, directions and identities. A major contribution to Irish studies.

THE IRISH MIND: Exploring Intellectual Traditions
Edited by RICHARD KEARNEY
366 pages · 216x138mm · ISBN 0 86327 047 6 PB

The now standard work on Irish intellectual and cultural development with contributions from thirteen leading scholars.

TRANSITIONS: Narratives in Modern Irish Culture
RICHARD KEARNEY
320 pages · 216x138mm · ISBN 0 86327 136 7 HB

'One of the sharpest and most intensely argued works on contemporary Irish culture.' *The Irish Times*

FR. BROWNE'S IRELAND:
Remarkable Images of People and Places
E. E. O'DONNELL
112 pages · 245x245mm · 140 photographs, text
ISBN 0 86327 200 2 HB

Superb duotone reproductions of photographs by Fr. Francis Browne sj, whose pictures are 'an unparalleled document of Irish life', and who 'by the close of this decade will be established as one of the great photographic talents of this century' (David H. Davison).

THE BOOK OF THE LIFFEY: from Source to the Sea
Edited by ELIZABETH HEALY.
Text by Gerard O'Flaherty, Christopher Moriarty
and other contributors
192 pages · 250x250mm · ISBN 0 86327 167 7 HB
Fully illustrated with colour and black and white.

Winner of the 1989 Irish Book Awards medal. A detailed illustrated narrative account of all aspects of the River Liffey, famed in literature. Opens and closes with Joycean colour sequences.

AUSTIN CLARKE: A Critical Introduction
MAURICE HARMON, MRAI
320 pages · 216x138mm · ISBN 0 86327 183 9 HB / 184 7 PB

An exciting re-evaluation of the achievement of Austin Clarke, this assessment by Dr. Harmon is an essential guide to the poems, plays and novels. Detailed bibliography, index. Portrait.

JOHN BANVILLE: A Critical Introduction
RÜDIGER IMHOF
224 pages · 216x138mm · ISBN 0 86327 186 3 HB / 187 1 PB

The first critical introduction to this exceptional novelist. Bibliography, index. Portrait.

JOSEPH CAMPBELL: A Critical Introduction
N. SAUNDERS & A. A. KELLY
Illustrated · 216x138mm · ISBN 0 86327 151 0 HB / 154 5 PB

Poet, patriot, composer, scholar, initiator of Irish studies in America, Joseph Campbell has been described as 'one of the rarest Gaelic minds of our time'.

THE MIRROR WALL
RICHARD MURPHY
ISBN 0 86327 220 7 HB / 221 5 PB

In Sri Lanka, a long wall of polished plaster, 'The Mirror Wall', bears twenty frescoes surviving since the fifth century, and is covered with graffiti – songs for love, satires, curses, celebrations. These were the inspiration for this powerful work. Illustrated with five colour reproductions and decorative emblems. (UK Bloodaxe Books; USA Wake Forest University Press).

(A fine edition, limited to 100 numbered copies world-wide, handbound, signed, and each including a handwritten poem by the poet (ISBN 0 86327 222 3 £125.00. Subscriptions in order of receipt. Available only from Wolfhound Press).

CARNIVAL
SEAMUS CASHMAN
ISBN 0 86327 127 8 cased · 129 4 PB

Poetry Wales on this first collection wrote: 'Pursuing a recurring theme in Carnival, the idea of a journey to the great beyond' . . . some of the best writing comes in the prose poems . . . 'Cast Shadows' and 'Fisheye Lens' are particularly beautiful examples of the genre . . . poems of lasting quality . . . a range of themes and issues.'

JOYCE'S DUBLIN: A Walking Guide to Ulysses
JACK McCARTHY with DANIS ROSE
Illustrated with maps and photos, fully revised 1988 edition.
ISBN 0 86327 169 3

THE JOYCEAN WAY: A Topographical Guide to DUBLINERS and A PORTRAIT
BRUCE BIDWELL & LINDA HEFFER
144 pages · 246x170mm · ISBN 0 86327 173 1

Extensive text, detailed maps, photographs; glossary of place-names; bibliography. Paperback edition June 1991.

THE ANNALS OF DUBLIN – FAIR CITY
E. E. O'DONNELL sj
240 pages · 250x180mm · illustrated · ISBN 0 86327 149 9 HB

'E. E. O'Donnell's fascinating chronology of Dublin is one of the best publications ever produced about the capital.'
Evening Herald

A SHORT HISTORY OF ANGLO-IRISH LITERATURE
MAURICE HARMON & ROGER McHUGH
384 pages · illustrations · 216x138mm · ISBN 0 905473 52 3 HB

An outstanding critical introduction to and history of literature in Ireland.

THE IRISH COUNTRYSIDE:
Landscape, Wildlife, History, People
Edited by DESMOND GILLMOR
240 pages · 234x155mm · illustrated · ISBN 0 86327 159 6 PB

A welcome book for the general reader by leading geographers.